Gospel

Gospel

THE UNFORGETTABLE STORY

edited by Donald de Beer

Fount
An Imprint of HarperCollins*Publishers*

HarperCollins*Religious*
part of HarperCollins*Publishers*
77–85 Fulham Palace Road, London W6 8JB
www.**fire**and**water**.com

First published in Great Britain in 2000 by
HarperCollins*Publishers*

1 3 5 7 9 10 8 6 4 2

A catalogue record for this book
is available from the British Library.

Imprimatur
In accordance with canon 825 §1 of the Code of Canon Law, the
Southern African Catholic Bishops' Conference has approved
the publication *Gospel*, submitted by the Rt Rev Monsignor
Donald de Beer.

ISBN 0 00 628161 3

Printed and bound in Great Britain by
Clays Ltd, St Ives plc

CONTENTS

WHAT THIS BOOK OFFERS YOU

This book combines the four gospels of Matthew, Mark, Luke and John into one, with nothing added and nothing left out, and puts what they tell us into the order in which the events probably took place. Instead of reading two, three or four separate versions of the same episode, you read just one that is more complete than any of them.

Scripture scholars have to study the separate gospels: their differences, and the way they relate to one another. But even they may exaggerate those differences when they say it is impossible to reconcile them.

For example, one gospel writer will say there was one blind man or one leper when another says there were two. But so long as the first doesn't say there was *only* one, there is no contradiction. There were two, but one of them was more important for some reason.

Another example: St Matthew writes as though Jesus, Mary and Joseph settled in Nazareth only after the flight into Egypt. If he actually said this, he would contradict St Luke's account.

But in fact he doesn't deny what Luke tells us; perhaps he just didn't know.

Again, there seems to be a real contradiction when the gospels tell us how Jesus sent his twelve apostles on a mission (page 78): Matthew says he told them not to take sandals or a staff, while Mark makes him say they should. But when you put their accounts together, it seems clear that he told them not to take a *spare* pair of sandals or staff, just as he told them not to take a second tunic. They were to have only what they needed at any time, but he didn't tell them to go barefoot.

You will find some of these things explained in footnotes, in case you're interested. But what strikes me most is the way the gospel writers complete one another, especially the way St John avoids repeating what the others have reported – the institution of the Eucharist, for instance – but adds important things they left out, like what Jesus said about his presence in the Eucharist (pages 84 to 87).

May this book make Jesus and what he said and did more vividly alive for you, as writing it did for me. I have to take responsibility for the way the Greek texts have been put into English. I know almost no Greek, so I relied on a dictionary and a word-for-word translation by the Rev. Alfred Marshall (*The Interlinear Greek-English New Testament*, Samuel Bagster & Sons, 1967) and often looked at the New Revised Standard Version and the New Jerusalem Bible to see how they translate a word or a phrase; then I made up my own mind.

I had hoped to make the English as literal as possible, but soon learned that the four gospels were not written with classical precision or economy of words. They are the inspired word of

God in the words of ordinary men, and since what I was doing was essentially an editing job, I have sometimes dared to tighten up the sacred texts. Although *Gospel* leaves nothing out, it does prune a few of St John's repetitions.

Gospel

ST LUKE SAYS THIS IS GENUINE HISTORY

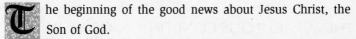 any have undertaken to write accounts of the deeds accomplished among us, according to the testimony of those who were eyewitnesses and servants of the Word from the beginning. So I thought I should do the same for you, most excellent Theophilus, after I had carefully investigated everything at its source, so that you could be certain of the truth of the things you were taught.

(LUKE 1:1–14)

JESUS, SON OR WORD OF THE FATHER

he beginning of the good news about Jesus Christ, the Son of God.

From all eternity, the Word was with God, and the Word was God. Everything was created through him, and nothing without him. In him was life, and this life was the light of men. It shines in the dark, and the darkness has not overcome it.

There was a man sent by God whose name was John. He was not that light which enlightens everyone who comes into the world, but he came to bear witness to him, so that everyone could believe through him.

The true light came into a world which had come into being through him, yet it did not recognize him. He came to what was his own, and his own people would not accept him. But to those who did believe in him he gave the right to become children of God, born not of blood nor the will of the flesh nor the will of man, but from God himself.

The Word was made flesh, and pitched his tent among us; and we saw his glory, the glory of the Father's only Son, full of grace and truth.

John bore witness to him, calling out: 'This is the man of whom I said: "The one coming after me comes before me, because he existed before me."' Indeed, we have all received our existence from him, and gift upon gift; the law was given through Moses, but grace and truth through Jesus Christ. No man has ever seen God; but God the Son, in the bosom of the Father, has made him known.

(MARK 1:1; JOHN 1:1–18)

THE MIRACULOUS CONCEPTION OF JOHN THE BAPTIST

In the time of King Herod of Judaea, there was a priest named Zechariah of the order of Abijah whose wife Elizabeth belonged to the tribe of Aaron. Both were virtuous in God's sight, blameless in keeping all the Lord's commandments and ordinances. But they had no child, because they were old and Elizabeth had always been sterile.

While Zechariah was doing his priestly duty before God during the turn of his order, it fell to him, according to the custom of the priesthood, to go into the sanctuary of the Lord at the time appointed for burning incense, while the congregation prayed outside.

An angel of the Lord appeared to him, standing at the right of the altar of incense. Seeing this vision, Zechariah was disturbed, and fear took hold of him. But the angel said: 'Zechariah, don't be afraid; your prayer has been heard, and your wife Elizabeth will bear you a son.

'You are to call him John, and he will bring you joy and gladness. Many will rejoice at his birth, because he will be great in the eyes of the Lord.

'He must never drink wine or spirits. From his mother's womb he will be filled with the Holy Spirit, and will turn many sons of Israel to the Lord. He will go before God in the spirit and power of Elijah, to prepare the people for the Lord; to turn the hearts of fathers to their children, and teach sinners the wisdom that honest people have.'

But Zechariah said to the angel: 'How can I believe this? I am old, and so is my wife.'

The angel answered: 'I am Gabriel who stands before God, and I was sent to speak to you and tell you these things. Since you have not believed my words, which will be fulfilled in their time, here is a proof for you: you will be dumb till the day your son is born.'

Meanwhile the people were waiting for Zechariah, wondering why he stayed so long in the sanctuary. When he came out, he could not speak to them. He made signs to them but remained speechless, and they understood he had seen a vision in the sanctuary.

When the days of his service were over he went home to his house, and soon after that his wife Elizabeth conceived. She kept to herself for five months, saying: 'The Lord did this for me when he looked on me favourably and took away my reproach among men.'

(LUKE 1:5–25)

THE MIRACULOUS CONCEPTION OF JESUS

n the sixth month of the year, the angel Gabriel was sent by God to a town in Galilee called Nazareth, to a virgin promised in marriage to a descendant of David named Joseph. The virgin's name was Mary.

Coming in, he said to her: 'Hail, favoured one, the Lord is with you.' When she heard this she was greatly disturbed, and wondered what sort of greeting it was.

But the angel said: 'Mary, don't be afraid; you have found favour with God. Listen: you are about to conceive in your womb and bear a son. You are to call him Jesus; he will be great, and will be called Son of the Most High. The Lord God will give him the throne of his ancestor David, and he will reign over the house of Jacob for ever; of his kingdom there will be no end.'

Then Mary asked the angel: 'How will this happen, since I have no intercourse with a man?'

The angel answered: 'The Holy Spirit will come upon you, and the power of the Most High will overshadow you. For this reason the Holy One you will bear will be called Son of God.

'And listen, your cousin Elizabeth has also conceived a son in her old age. The one they called barren is six months pregnant, because nothing is impossible to God.'

Then Mary said: 'I am the Lord's servant; let what you have said be done to me.' And the angel left her.

(LUKE 1:26–38)

Two partial[1] lists of the human ancestors of Jesus

A record of the lineage of Jesus Christ, son of David and son of Abraham:

God

Adam

Seth

Enos

Cainan

Mahalaleel

Jared

Enoch

Methuselah

Lamech

Noah

Shem

Arphaxad

Cainan

Shelah

Eber

Peleg

Reu

Serug

Nahor

Terah

Abraham
Isaac
Jacob
Judah (and his brothers)
Perez (and Zerah, by Tamar)
Hezron
Arni, Aram, Admin (and others)
Amminadab
Nahshon
Salmon or Sala
Boaz (by Rahab)
Obed (by Ruth)
Jesse
King David

Solomon (by Uriah's wife)	Nathan
Rehoboam	Mattatha
Abijah	Menna
Asaph or Asa	Melea
Jehoshaphat	Eliakim
Joram	Jonam
...	Joseph
Uzziah	Judah
Jotham	Simeon
Ahaz	Levi
Hezekiah	Matthat
Manasseh	Jorim
Amos or Amon	Eliezer

Josiah	Joshua
Jechoniah	Er
(and his brothers,	Elmadam
at the time of	Cosam
the deportation	Addi
to Babylon)	Melchi
Neri	

Salathiel or Shealtiel
Zerubbabel

Abiud	Rhesa
Joanan	
Eliakim	Joda
Josech	
Azor	Semein
Mattathias	
Zadok	Maath
Naggai	
Achim	Esli
Nahum	
Eliud	Amos
Mattathias	
Eleazar	Joseph
Jannai	
Matthan	Melchi
Levi	

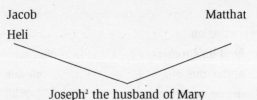

Jacob   Matthat

Heli

Joseph² the husband of Mary

Jesus called Christ, who was regarded as the son of Joseph

(MATTHEW 1:1–16; LUKE 3:23–38)

MARY VISITS HER COUSIN ELIZABETH

At this time Mary set out and hurried to a town in the hill country of Judaea, where she went into the house of Zechariah and greeted Elizabeth; and as soon as Elizabeth heard Mary's greeting, the baby leapt in her womb.

Elizabeth was filled with the Holy Spirit; she called out with a loud cry and said: 'Blessed are you among women, and blessed is the fruit of your womb! What have I done to deserve a visit from the mother of my Lord? I tell you, when the sound of your greeting came to my ears, the baby in my womb jumped for joy. Blessed is she who believed, because the promises given her from the Lord will be fulfilled.'

Then Mary said: 'My soul praises the Lord, and my spirit exults in God my Saviour for looking on his servant's humility. See, from now on all generations will call me blessed, because the Almighty has done great things to me. Holy is his name, and his mercy is for those who fear him in every generation.

'He has shown the strength of his arm; he has scattered those who thought themselves high and mighty. He has pulled those in power down from their thrones, and raised up the humble. He has filled the hungry with good things and sent the rich away empty. He has come to the help of Israel his servant, remembering the mercy he promised to our ancestors, to Abraham and his descendants for ever.'

Mary stayed with Elizabeth for about three months and then returned to her house.

(LUKE 1:39–56)

THE BIRTH OF JOHN THE BAPTIST

ow the time came for Elizabeth to give birth, and she bore a son. Her neighbours and relatives heard that the Lord had shown her this great mercy and rejoiced with her. On the eighth day they came to circumcise the child and name him Zechariah after his father. But his mother said: 'No; he shall be called John.' They said to her: 'There is no one in your family who has this name,' and turned to the father to see what he wanted to call the child. Asking for a tablet, Zechariah wrote: 'John is his name,' and they all marvelled; and at once Zechariah began to speak, praising and thanking God.

Fear came on all who lived in the neighbourhood, and the news was talked about throughout the hill country of Judaea. All who heard it kept it in mind and wondered what this child would become; they were sure the hand of the Lord was on him. And his father Zechariah was filled with the Holy Spirit, and prophesied in these words:

'Blessed be the Lord, the God of Israel, who has visited his people to redeem them. As he promised long ago through his holy prophets, he has raised up among the descendants of his servant David a power of salvation for us, salvation from our enemies and the hands of all who hate us.

'He has shown us the mercy he promised our ancestors, and remembered his holy covenant, the oath he swore to our father Abraham that he would save us from the hands of our enemies to serve him without fear, living all our days in holiness and righteousness in his presence.

'And you, child, will be called a prophet of the Most High, because you will go before the Lord to prepare his ways. Out of the depth of the mercy of our God you will let his people know salvation through the forgiveness of their sins. And he will send a rising sun from heaven to visit us, to shine on those living in darkness and in the shadow of death, and guide our feet into the way of peace.'

The child grew and became strong in spirit. He stayed in desert places until he began to make himself known to Israel.

(LUKE 1:57–80)

THE BIRTH OF JESUS

his is how Jesus the Messiah was born. While his mother was still engaged to Joseph, before they came together, she was found to be pregnant by the Holy Spirit.

Her husband Joseph, a fair man who did not wish to make an example of her, decided to break off from her privately. But while he was thinking this over an angel of the Lord appeared to him in a dream and said:

'Joseph son of David, do not be afraid to take Mary as your wife, because the child conceived in her is of the Holy Spirit. She will bear a son, and you shall name him Jesus, because he will save his people from their sins.

'This has happened in fulfilment of what the Lord said through the prophet: "The virgin will conceive in her womb and give birth to a son, and they will call him Emmanuel"' (which means 'God with us').

When Joseph had woken, he did as the angel had told him. He took Mary as his wife, but did not have intercourse with her; and after she had borne her son, he gave him the name Jesus.

But before that, a decree went out from Emperor Augustus ordering a census of the whole world. This first census took place while Quirinius was governing Syria.

Everyone went to his own town to be registered, so Joseph went up from Nazareth in Galilee to Bethlehem in Judaea – the city of David, because he was of the house and family of David – to be enrolled with Mary his pregnant spouse. It was while they were there that the time came for her to give birth.

She bore her firstborn son and wrapped him in swaddling-clothes, and laid him in a feeding-trough for animals because there was no room for them at the inn.

There were shepherds nearby, living in the fields, guarding their flocks at night. An angel of the Lord stood before them, and the glory of the Lord shone around them. They were terrified, but the angel said:

'Do not be afraid. Listen, I bring you news that will give great joy to everyone. Today a saviour, Christ the Lord, has been born to you in the city of David. And here is a sign for you: you will find the baby wrapped in swaddling-clothes, lying in a feeding-trough.'

Suddenly with the angel there was a host of the heavenly army, praising God and saying: 'Glory to God in highest heaven, and on earth peace to men of good will.' Then the angels went away from them into heaven.

The shepherds said to one another: Let us go to Bethlehem, then, and see what has happened, this thing that the Lord has made known to us. Hurrying, they came and found Mary and Joseph, and the baby lying in the feeding-trough.

When the shepherds saw them, they repeated what they had been told about this child, and all who heard it marvelled. But Mary kept these things to herself, pondering them in her heart. The shepherds returned, glorifying and praising God for all the things they had heard and seen, just as they had been told.

(MATTHEW 1:18–25; LUKE 2:1–20)

THE CIRCUMCISION AND PRESENTATION OF JESUS

After eight days it was time to circumcise the child, and his father named him Jesus, the name the angel had given him before he was conceived. And when, according to the law of Moses, the days of their purification were completed, his parents took him up to Jerusalem to present him to the Lord, as prescribed in the law of the Lord: 'Every male that opens the womb shall be called sacred to the Lord.' And they offered the sacrifice the law prescribes, a pair of turtle-doves or two young pigeons.

Now there was a man in Jerusalem named Simeon, just and devout, who looked forward to the consolation of Israel; and the Holy Spirit was upon him. It had been made known to him by the Holy Spirit that he would not see death before he saw the Lord's anointed one.

The Spirit led him into the temple just as the parents of Jesus brought in their child to do for him what the law prescribes. Simeon took him in his arms and blessed God, and said: 'Now, Master, you are letting your servant go in peace as you promised, because my eyes have seen the salvation which you have prepared in the sight of all peoples: a light of revelation for the gentiles, and the glory of your people Israel.'

His father and mother marvelled at what was being said about him. Simeon blessed them, and said to Mary: 'Listen: this child will be the occasion for the falling and rising again of many in Israel. He will be a sign that many will contradict, revealing their own secret thoughts; and a sword will pierce your own soul too.'

There was also Anna, a prophetess, the daughter of Phanuel of the tribe of Asher. After her virginity she had lived with her husband for seven years, and was now a widow of eighty-four who never left the temple, serving God night and day with fasting and prayer. Coming upon them at that moment, she gave thanks to God, and talked about the child to everyone who looked forward to the redemption of Jerusalem.

When Mary and Joseph had done everything according to the law of the Lord, they returned to Galilee, to their town of Nazareth.

(LUKE 2:21–39; MATTHEW 1:25B)

THE COMING OF THE MAGI

After Jesus was born in Bethlehem in Judaea, in the time of King Herod, magi from the east arrived in Jerusalem, asking: 'Where is the one born to be king of the Jews? We have seen his star in the east, and have come to worship him.'

Hearing this, King Herod was troubled, and all Jerusalem with him. He assembled all the chief priests and scribes of the people and enquired of them where the Messiah would be born.

They told him it would be in Bethlehem in Judaea, because this was what the prophet had written: 'You, Bethlehem in the land of Judah, are by no means least among the leaders of Judah, because from you will come a ruler who will shepherd my people Israel.'

Then Herod summoned the magi in private and questioned them carefully about the time when the star had appeared. He sent them on to Bethlehem, saying: 'Go and make careful enquiries about the child. When you find him, report to me, so that I too may come and worship him.'

Having listened to the king they went on their way, and again they saw the star they had seen in the east. It went before them until it came to a halt over the place where the child was. When they saw this, they were filled with joy.

Coming into the house, they saw the child with Mary his mother. Falling to their knees they worshipped him, and opening their treasures offered him gifts of gold, incense and myrrh.

Then, having been warned by a dream not to return to Herod, they left for their own country by a different route.

(MATTHEW 2:1–12)

JESUS ESCAPES THE MASSACRE OF THE INNOCENTS

When the magi had left, an angel of the Lord appeared to Joseph in a dream and said: 'Get up, take the child and his mother and escape into Egypt, and stay there until I tell you, because Herod is going to look for the child to destroy him.'

So Joseph took the child and his mother and left for Egypt that night, and stayed there until Herod had died. In this way the words spoken by the Lord through the prophet were fulfilled: 'I called my son out of Egypt.'

Herod was enraged when he realized that the magi had fooled him, and sent his men to kill all male children up to two years old in Bethlehem and its districts, going by the time he had carefully ascertained from the magi. So the words spoken through the prophet Jeremiah were fulfilled: 'A voice was heard in Rama, weeping and loudly lamenting: Rachel wept for her children and would not be comforted, because they were no more.'

Then, when Herod himself had died, an angel of the Lord appeared to Joseph in a dream, saying: 'Get up, take the child and his mother and go back to the land of Israel, because those who wanted to kill the child are dead.' So he took the child and his mother and returned to the land of Israel.

But when he heard that Archelaus was ruling Judaea in succession to Herod his father, he was afraid to go there; and being warned by a dream, he headed for the district of Galilee and settled in a town called Nazareth, fulfilling what was said through the prophets: 'He shall be called a Nazarene.' And the child grew and became strong; he was filled with wisdom, and the grace of God was upon him.

(MATTHEW 2:13–23; LUKE 2:40)

JESUS LOST AND FOUND IN THE TEMPLE

The parents of Jesus went to Jerusalem every year for the feast of Passover. When he was twelve years old, they went up and took part in the festival days according to custom. But when they left to return home, the boy Jesus remained in Jerusalem without their knowledge.

They supposed he was among their group of pilgrims, and went a day's journey before they looked for him among their relatives and acquaintances. When they did not find him, they went back to Jerusalem to search for him.

After three days they found him in the temple, sitting among the teachers, listening to them and asking them questions; and all who heard him were amazed at his intelligence and the answers he gave.

His parents were astonished, and his mother said to him:

'Child, why did you do this to us? Look how upset your father and I have been, trying to find you.' But Jesus answered: 'Why is it that you looked for me? Didn't you know that I have to be busy with my Father's affairs?' They did not understand what he said.

So he went down with them and came to Nazareth, and was obedient to them. His mother carefully kept everything he said in her heart, and Jesus grew in wisdom, maturity and favour with God and man.

(LUKE 2:41–52)

JOHN BEGINS TO PREACH AND BAPTIZE

I n the fifteenth year of the reign of the emperor Tiberius, Pontius Pilate was governing Judaea and Herod ruled as tetrarch of Galilee. His brother Philip was tetrarch of the region of Ituraea and Trachonitis; Lysanias was tetrarch of Abilene.

In the time of the high priests Annas and Caiaphas, the word of God came to Zechariah's son, John the Baptizer. He appeared in the desert of Judaea, proclaiming to all in the Jordan region a baptism of repentance for forgiveness of sins.

He said: 'Repent, all of you, because the kingdom of heaven has come close.' And the inhabitants of all the country of Judaea, of Jerusalem and of the Jordan region came to confess their sins and be baptized by him in the Jordan river.

John dressed in camel hair with a leather belt round his waist, and his food was locusts and wild honey. He was the one foretold through the prophet Isaiah, as is written in the book of his teaching: 'See, I send my messenger before your face to prepare your way, a voice crying in the desert: "Prepare the way of the Lord; make his paths straight. Every valley must be filled up, every mountain and hill laid low. The crooked paths must be straightened and the rough ways made smooth, and all peoples shall see the salvation that comes from God."'

Among the crowds coming out to be baptized by him were many of the Pharisees and Sadducees. When he saw them, he said: 'Brood of vipers, who has warned you to escape from the wrath to come? Then produce the proper fruits of repentance, and don't think of saying to each other, "We are descended from Abraham," because I tell you, God can raise up children to Abraham out of these stones.

'Even now, the axe is being laid to the root of the trees; every tree that does not produce good fruit is being cut down and thrown on the fire.'

The crowds asked him: 'Then what should we do?' He answered them: 'Let anyone who has two tunics share with someone who has none, and let anyone who has food do the same.'

Tax collectors also came to be baptized, and said to him: 'Teacher, what should we do?' He said to them: 'Do no more than you have been ordered to do.'

Men serving in the army also asked: 'And we, what should we do?' He told them: 'Do not intimidate anyone; do not make false accusations, and be satisfied with your pay.'

(MATTHEW 3:1–10; MARK 1:2–6A; LUKE 3:3–14)

JOHN PROCLAIMS THE COMING MESSIAH

T̲heir expectations aroused, the people were now debating inwardly whether John himself might be the Christ. He responded by declaring openly: 'I have indeed baptized you with water for repentance; but one more powerful than I is coming after me. I am not fit to carry his sandals or bend down to loosen their thongs.

'He will baptize you with the Holy Spirit, and with fire. His winnowing fork is in his hand; he will thoroughly clean his threshing floor and gather the wheat into his barn, but the chaff he will burn with unquenchable fire.'

In this way he announced the good news to the people, admonishing them about many different things.

(MATTHEW 3:11–12; MARK 1:7–8; LUKE 3:15–18)

THE BAPTISM OF JESUS

W̲hen all the people had been baptized, Jesus came to John from Nazareth in Galilee to be baptized by him in the Jordan. But John refused, saying: 'I need to be baptized by you, and you come to me?'

Jesus answered: 'Let it be so. It is right that in this way we do everything that ought to be done.' Then John consented.

When Jesus had been baptized he came straight out of the water and was praying, when he saw the heavens torn open and the Spirit of God coming down on him in bodily form, like a dove. And a voice was heard coming out of the heavens: 'You are my son, the beloved, in whom I am well pleased.'

(MATTHEW 3:13–17; MARK 1:9–11; LUKE 3:21–2)

THE TEMPTATION OF JESUS

Jesus returned from the Jordan filled with the Holy Spirit, and at once the Spirit drove him into the desert to be tempted by Satan, the devil. He lived among wild animals and fasted, eating nothing for forty days and forty nights; and when they were over, he was hungry.

So the tempter came to him and said: 'If you are the Son of God, order these stones to change into loaves of bread.' But Jesus answered him: 'Scripture says: "Man shall not live on bread alone, but on every word that comes from the mouth of God."'

Then the devil took him into the holy city, Jerusalem, and set him on the pinnacle of the temple, saying: 'If you are Son of God, throw yourself down from here, because scripture says: "He will order his angels to protect you, and they will carry you in their hands so that you do not even hit your foot on a stone."' Jesus answered: 'Scripture also says: "You shall not put the Lord your God to the test."'

Again, the devil took him up an exceedingly high mountain and showed him in a moment all the kingdoms of the world and all their glory, and said: 'I will give you all these kingdoms, their power and their glory, because they have been surrendered to me and to whoever I wish to give them; all will be yours, on condition that you kneel and worship me.' Then Jesus answered him: 'Go, Satan, because scripture says: "You shall worship the Lord your God, and serve him alone."'

After that the devil gave up testing him and left him for a time, and angels came and looked after him.

(MATTHEW 4:1–11; MARK 1:12–13; LUKE 4:1–13)

JOHN SAYS WHO HE IS

This is the testimony John gave when the Jews sent priests and Levites from Jerusalem to ask him: 'Who are you?' He did not refuse to reply, but said openly: 'I am not the Christ.' Then they asked him: 'Who then: are you Elijah?' And he said: 'I am not.' 'Are you the prophet?' And he answered: 'No.'

So they said to him: 'Who are you? Give us an answer we can take to those who sent us. What do you say about yourself?'

He answered: 'I am the voice of one crying in the desert: "Make straight the way of the Lord," as Isaiah the prophet said.'

Those who had been sent were Pharisees. They questioned him again: 'Why do you baptize, if you are not the Christ, nor Elijah, nor the prophet?'

John answered: 'I only baptize in water; but among you stands someone you do not know – the one coming after me whose sandal thong I am not worthy to untie.'

These things happened in Bethany beyond the Jordan, where John was baptizing.

(JOHN 1:19–28)

'THIS IS THE LAMB OF GOD'

The next day, John saw Jesus coming towards him, and said: 'Look! This is the Lamb of God who takes away the sin of the world.

'This is the one of whom I said: "After me comes a man who ranks before me, because he existed before me." And I did not know him, but the reason I came baptizing with water was so that he could be manifested to Israel.

'He who sent me to baptize in water said to me: "The one on whom you see the Spirit come down and rest, this is the one who baptizes in the Holy Spirit." I saw this, and have testified that this man is the Son of God.'

(JOHN 1:29–34)

JESUS CALLS HIS FIRST DISCIPLES

Again the next day John was standing with two of his disciples and saw Jesus walking by. He said: 'Look, the Lamb of God!' The two disciples heard this, and followed Jesus.

Turning to them, Jesus asked: 'What are you looking for?' They said to him: 'Rabbi [teacher], where do you stay?' He answered: 'Come and see.' So they went and saw where he stayed and spent that day with him; it was about four in the afternoon.

Andrew, Simon Peter's brother, was one of the two who heard what John said and followed Jesus. Andrew first found

Simon and told him: 'We have found the Messiah' (the Christ, the anointed one), and led him to Jesus. Looking at him, Jesus said: 'You are Simon, son of John; you will be called Cephas' or Peter (both names mean rock).

The day after that Jesus wanted to go into Galilee when he found Philip, and said to him: 'Follow me.' Philip was from Bethsaida, the town of Andrew and Peter.

Philip then found Nathanael and told him: 'We have found the one that Moses wrote about in the law, and the prophets too: he is Jesus, son of Joseph, from Nazareth.' Nathanael said: 'Can anything good come out of Nazareth?' Philip said to him: 'Come and see.'

Jesus saw Nathanael coming towards him and said of him: 'Look, a true Israelite in whom there is no guile.' Nathanael said to him: 'From where do you know me?' Jesus answered: 'Before Philip called you, I saw you under the fig tree.' Nathanael answered him: 'Rabbi, you really are the Son of God; you are the King of Israel!'

Jesus responded: 'Do you believe this because I told you that I saw you under the fig tree? You will see greater things than these.' And he added: 'Truly I tell you, you will see heaven opened, and the angels of God going up and coming down upon the Son of Man.'

(JOHN 1:35-51)

JESUS TURNS WATER INTO WINE

n the third day there was a wedding at Cana in Galilee, and the mother of Jesus was there. Jesus and his disciples were also invited.

When the wine ran out, his mother told him: 'They have no wine.' He answered: 'Woman, what is that to us? My hour has not yet come.' But his mother said to the servants: 'Do whatever he tells you.'

There were six stone water jars standing there for the Jewish purifications, each of which held thirty or forty-five litres. Jesus told the servants: 'Fill the jars with water,' and they filled them to the brim. Then he said: 'Now draw some out and take it to the chief steward,' and they did.

When the steward tasted the water, it had turned into wine and he did not know where it had come from, though the servants who had drawn the water knew.

So the steward called the bridegroom and said: 'Everyone serves the good wine first, and the wine that is not so good when people get drunk; but you have kept the good wine till now.'

Jesus worked this first miracle at Cana in Galilee, and revealed his glory, and his disciples believed in him. Then he went down to Capernaum with his mother, his brothers and his disciples, but did not stay there long.

(JOHN 2:1–12)

JESUS EXPELS THE TRADERS FROM THE TEMPLE

When the Jewish Passover was near, Jesus went up to Jerusalem. Entering the temple, he found money-changers and those who bought and sold oxen, sheep and doves.

Making a whip out of cords, he began driving them out of the temple with their sheep and oxen. He overturned the seats of the sellers of doves and the tables of the money-changers, spilling their coins, and told them: 'Take these things out of here, and stop turning my Father's house into a market.' He would not allow anyone to carry so much as a jar through the temple.

Teaching them, he said: 'Doesn't scripture tell us: "My house shall be called a house of prayer for all the nations"? But you have made it a den of robbers.' And his disciples remembered another text: 'Zeal for your house will consume me.'

The Jews responded by asking him: 'What warrant can you show us for doing these things?' Jesus answered: 'Destroy this shrine, and I will raise it up in three days.'

They protested: 'It took forty-six years to build this shrine, and will you raise it in three days?' But Jesus was talking about the shrine that was his body. When he was raised from the dead, his disciples remembered that he had said this, and believed both the scripture and what he had said.

When it became late they left the city. But he taught daily in the temple, and the chief priests and scribes and leading laymen heard about it. They wanted to destroy him but could not find a way, because the people hung on his words. They were astonished by his teaching.

27

While he was in Jerusalem for the Passover feast, many saw the miracles he was working and came to believe in him. But Jesus did not commit himself to them, because he understood all men. He knew what is in man; he did not need anyone to tell him.

(MATTHEW 21:12–13; MARK 11:15–18; LUKE 19:45–8; JOHN 2:13–25)

JESUS TELLS NICODEMUS ABOUT THE BAPTISM HE WILL GIVE

There was one of the Pharisees called Nicodemus, a leading man among the Jews, who came to Jesus by night and said: 'Rabbi, we know you are a teacher who has come from God, because no one could do these miracles you work unless God were with him.'

Jesus answered: 'I tell you truly, unless someone is born from heaven, he cannot see the kingdom of God.'

Nicodemus said: 'How can someone be born when he is old? Surely he can't enter the womb of his mother a second time, and be born?'

Jesus answered: 'Truly I tell you, unless he is born from water and the Spirit, he cannot enter the kingdom of God. What is born of a woman is only human; what is born of the Spirit is spirit.

'Don't be surprised that I told you that you need to be born from heaven. The wind blows where it wants to, and you hear the sound of it, but you don't know where it comes from or where it is going; that is how it is with anyone born of the Spirit.'

Nicodemus asked: 'But how do such things come about?'

Jesus answered: 'You are a teacher in Israel, and do not know these things? I tell you truly, we tell what we know, and testify about what we have seen; but you do not accept our testimony. If I told you about earthly things and you did not believe me, how will you believe me when I tell you about heavenly things?

'No man has gone up to heaven except the one who has come down from heaven, the Son of Man. And as Moses lifted up the serpent in the desert, so must the Son of Man be lifted up, so that everyone who believes in him may have eternal life.

'God loved the world so much that he gave his only Son, so that whoever believes in him need not perish, but may have eternal life. God did not send his Son into the world to condemn it, but so that through him the world might be saved. Whoever believes in him is not condemned; but whoever does not believe is already condemned, because he has not believed in the person of God's only Son.

'And this is the judgement: that the light has come into the world, but men loved the darkness more than the light because their deeds were evil. Those who do evil things hate and avoid the light, for fear their sins will be exposed and condemned. But one who does what is right and good comes to the light, so that everyone can see that what he did was done in God.'

(JOHN 3:1–21)

MEANWHILE, JOHN'S BAPTISM CONTINUES

After this Jesus and his disciples came and baptized in the country of Judaea, though it was not Jesus himself who baptized, but his disciples; and he spent some time with them there. John, not yet imprisoned, was also baptizing in Aenon near Salim; there was plenty of water there, and people kept coming for baptism.

Because of this, a Jew questioned John's disciples about purification, and they came to John and said: 'Rabbi, the one who was with you beyond the Jordan, the one about whom you bore witness – he is also baptizing, and everyone is going to him.'

John answered: 'A man cannot receive anything unless it is given to him by heaven. You are witnesses that I said I was not the Messiah, but only the one sent before him.

'The bridegroom has the bride, but his friend who stands listening rejoices to hear his voice; this is why my joy is complete.

'He must grow greater, but I must grow less. He who comes from the earth belongs to the earth, and speaks of the earth; but the one who comes from heaven is above everything. He testifies to what he has seen and heard, but no one accepts his testimony. Whoever does accept his testimony accepts the truthfulness of God, because he whom God has sent speaks the words of God, who does not give the Spirit by measure.

'The Father loves the Son and has given all things into his hand. Whoever believes in the Son has eternal life. But no one who disobeys the Son will see life; the wrath of God remains on him.'

(JOHN 3:22–36; 4:2)

JOHN IS IMPRISONED

ohn had reproved Herod the tetrarch for marrying Herodias, his brother Philip's wife. After John told Herod it was against the law for him to have her and rebuked him for other evil things he did, Herod did his worst yet: he sent men to arrest John and shut him up in prison.

Herodias naturally had a grudge against John and wanted to kill him, but she could not do it because Herod protected him. Herod would also have liked to kill John, but he was afraid of him, knowing that he was a just and holy man; and he feared the crowd, because they regarded him as a prophet. Besides, he liked listening to John, though when he did he was greatly perplexed.

Jesus, hearing that John had been imprisoned, and knowing the Pharisees had heard that he made and baptized more disciples than John, left Judaea and returned to Galilee, filled with the power of the Spirit.

(MATTHEW 4:12; 14:3–5; MARK 1:14A; 6:17–20;
LUKE 3:19–20; 4:14A; JOHN 4:1,3)

JESUS AND THE SAMARITAN WOMAN: THE WATER OF LIFE

aving to pass through Samaria, Jesus came to a Samaritan town called Sychar near the piece of land Jacob gave his son Joseph, on which is Jacob's well. Wearied by the journey, he sat down there about midday while his disciples went into the town to buy food.

When a Samaritan woman came to draw water, he said to her: 'Give me a drink.' She replied: 'How can a Jew like you ask me, a Samaritan woman, for a drink?' Jews do not associate with Samaritans.

Jesus answered: 'If you knew the gift of God and who it is that is asking you for a drink, you would have asked him, and he would have given you living water.'

She said: 'Sir, you have no bucket, and the well is deep. Where do you get living water? Surely you are not greater than our father Jacob, who gave us this well, and drank from it himself, and his sons and his cattle?'

Jesus answered her: 'Whoever drinks this water will soon be thirsty again. But one who drinks the water I give will never thirst again; it will become a spring inside him, and the source of eternal life.'

The woman said: 'Sir, give me this water, so that I never get thirsty and never have to come here to draw water.'

Then Jesus said to her: 'Go and call your husband and come back here.'

She answered: 'I have no husband.'

Jesus replied: 'You may well say you have no husband, because you have had five, and the man with you now is not your husband. You told the truth there.'

So the woman said to him: 'Sir, it seems to me you are a prophet! But our fathers worshipped on this mountain, and you Jews say that Jerusalem is the place where one must worship.'

Jesus said to her: 'Believe me, woman, a time is coming when you will worship the Father neither on this mountain nor in Jerusalem. You Samaritans do not know what you worship; we know, because salvation comes from the Jews.

'But a time is coming – in fact it is here already – when true worshippers will worship the Father in spirit and in truth. These are the ones whose worship the Father seeks. God is Spirit, and those who worship must worship in spirit and truth.'

The woman said: 'I know that the Messiah is coming,' the Christ, 'and when he comes, he will tell us everything.' Then Jesus said to her: 'I am he, the one speaking to you.'

At this his disciples returned, surprised to find him speaking with a woman; but no one asked: 'What are you looking for?' or 'Why are you talking to her?'

The woman left her water jar, went back to the town and said to the men: 'Come and see a man who has told me everything I have done; he couldn't be the Messiah, could he?' And they came out of the town to him.

In the meantime the disciples said to him: 'Rabbi, eat.' But he answered: 'I have food to eat that you do not know about.' They said to one another: 'Surely no one has brought him food?' But Jesus said: 'My food is to do the will of the one who sent me, and to finish his work.

'Haven't you a saying: Four months till the harvest? But open your eyes, look at the fields; they're already white for harvesting. Already the reaper is taking his wages and gathering fruit for eternal life, so that sower and reaper rejoice together.

'To this the proverb applies: One man sows, another reaps. I sent you to reap what you have not worked for; others have done it, and you have come into their work.'

Many of the Samaritans who lived in that town believed in Jesus on the testimony of the woman: 'He told me everything I have done.' So when they spoke to him, they asked him to stay with them, and he stayed there two days. Many more believed because of the things he said. They told the woman: 'We no longer believe because of what you said; we ourselves have listened to him, and we are sure that this man is the Saviour of the world.'

(JOHN 4:4–42)

IN GALILEE, JESUS CURES THE COURTIER'S SON

After two days Jesus went on into Galilee. He himself had pointed out that a prophet has no honour in his own birthplace, but when he returned to Galilee the Galileans received him well, because they too had attended the feast in Jerusalem and seen everything Jesus did there.

So he came again to Cana where he had turned the water into wine. There he met a courtier whose son was sick in Capernaum. When the courtier heard that Jesus had come back from Judaea to Galilee, he approached him and asked him to come and cure his son, who seemed about to die.

Jesus said: 'You never believe unless you see wonders and miracles.'

The courtier replied: 'Sir, come down before my child dies.'

Jesus told him: 'Go; your son will live.'

The man believed what Jesus told him, and went; and while he was on his way, his servants met him and told him the boy was alive.

34

He asked what time his son had got better, and they said: 'The fever left him yesterday afternoon at one o'clock.' The father knew that was when Jesus told him: 'Your son will live'; and he and his whole household believed.

This was the second miracle Jesus worked after returning from Judaea to Galilee.

(JOHN 4:43–54)

JESUS PREACHES IN NAZARETH AND CAPERNAUM

From then on Jesus began to teach in their synagogues, announcing the good news from God. He said: 'The time is here; repent, all of you, and believe in the gospel, because the kingdom of God has come close.' He was praised by everyone, and news of him spread throughout the country.

He came to Nazareth where he had been brought up. As his custom was, he went to the synagogue on the sabbath day and stood up to read. A scroll of the prophet Isaiah was handed to him, and he opened it and found the place where these words were written:

'The Spirit of the Lord is upon me; he has anointed me to bring good news to the poor. He has sent me to announce release to captives and sight to the blind, to let the oppressed go free, and to proclaim a year of favour from the Lord.'

When he had rolled up the scroll and given it back to the attendant, he sat down, and the eyes of all in the synagogue were fixed on him. Then he began to tell them: 'Today this scripture has been fulfilled in your hearing.'

Afterwards everyone praised him, marvelling at the words of grace he had spoken.

Leaving Nazareth, he went down and stayed in Capernaum, a coastal town in Galilee in the region of Zebulon and Naphtali, and at once began teaching them in the synagogue on the sabbath. The crowds were astonished by his teaching, because he spoke as one having authority, not the way their scribes taught them.

So he fulfilled what had been foretold through the prophet Isaiah: 'Land of Zebulon, land of Naphtali, way by the sea beyond the Jordan, Galilee of the gentiles: the people sitting in darkness have seen a great light, and on those who lived in the land and shadow of death, light has dawned.'

(MATTHEW 4:13–17; 7:28B–29; MARK 1:14B–15,21–2; LUKE 4:14B–22A,31–2)

A MIRACULOUS CATCH: JESUS CALLS PETER, ANDREW, JAMES AND JOHN

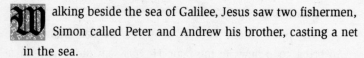 alking beside the sea of Galilee, Jesus saw two fishermen, Simon called Peter and Andrew his brother, casting a net in the sea.

Later, when a crowd was pressing around him to hear the word of God, he saw their two boats standing by the lake; the crews had left to wash the nets.

Getting into Simon's boat, Jesus asked him to put out a little from the land, and sitting in the boat he taught the crowds from there.

When he had finished speaking, he said to Simon: 'Put out into the deep, and drop your nets for a catch.' Simon answered: 'Master, we worked all night and took nothing. But if you say so, I will drop the nets.'

When they did this, they netted so many fish that the nets began to tear. They signalled to their partners in the other boat to come and help them, and filled both boats to sinking point.

When they saw the catch of fish, astonishment seized Simon Peter and all those with him; among them were his partners James and John, Zebedee's sons.

Simon fell at the knees of Jesus and said: 'Lord, leave me: I am a sinful man.' But Jesus said to him: 'Don't be afraid; from now on you will be catching living men.'

Going a little further he saw James and his brother John in the boat with their father, mending their nets. At once he called them, saying: 'Follow me, and I will make you fishers of men.'

They brought the boats to land, left their father Zebedee in the boat with the crew and the nets and at once became followers of Jesus.

(MATTHEW 4:18–22; MARK 1:16–20; LUKE 5:1–11)

JESUS FREES A MAN POSSESSED BY A DEMON

I n the synagogue at Capernaum there was a man possessed by an unclean spirit. Loudly he jeered: 'Jesus of Nazareth, what is your business with us? Have you come to destroy us? I know who you are; the holy one of God.'

Jesus rebuked the demon, saying: 'Be quiet; come out of him.' And the demon threw the man to the ground among all the people and came out of him with a loud shout, not injuring him at all.

Then they were all astonished, asking one another how Jesus could speak this way, teaching new things with authority and giving orders to unclean spirits, making them obey him and go. The news about him spread rapidly to every place in the region of Galilee.

(MARK 1:23–8; LUKE 4:33–7)

JESUS HEALS PETER'S MOTHER-IN-LAW AND MANY OTHERS

When they left the synagogue, Jesus and James and John went into the house of Simon Peter and Andrew. They told him that Simon's mother-in-law had been put to bed with a high fever, and asked him to help her.

He came and stood over her, touched her hand, rebuked the fever and lifted her up. At once the fever left her and she got up and served them.

When evening came, the whole town assembled at the door; they brought him all who were suffering from different diseases, and he laid his hands on each of them and healed them. In this way he fulfilled what had been foretold through Isaiah the prophet: 'He took our infirmities and bore our diseases.'

They also brought him many who were possessed by demons. He expelled the spirits with a word, and they came out shouting: 'You are the Son of God.' But he rebuked the demons and did not allow them to speak, because they knew he was the Christ.

(MATTHEW 8:14–17; MARK 1:29–34; LUKE 4:38–41)

JESUS LEAVES CAPERNAUM TO SPREAD THE GOSPEL

G etting up while it was still dark, Jesus went out at day-break to a desert place and prayed. Simon and the crowds that were with him searched for him, and when they found him, said: 'Everyone is looking for you.'

They wanted to prevent him from leaving them. But he said: 'Let us go somewhere else. I have to visit all the towns around here to preach the kingdom of God, because that is why I came; that is why I was sent.'

So he went about the whole of Galilee teaching in their syn-agogues, proclaiming the good news of the kingdom, driving out demons, and healing the people of every disease and sickness.

(MATTHEW 4:23; MARK 1:35–9; LUKE 4:42–4)

THE HEALING OF A LEPER

W hile he was in one of the towns a man came to him cov-ered with leprosy and knelt in worship and begged: 'Lord, if you are willing, I know you can cure me.'

Filled with tenderness, Jesus stretched out his hand and touched him, saying: 'I am willing; be healed.' The leprosy left him at once and he was cured.

Then Jesus sternly ordered him: 'Go away and don't say anything to anyone. Just show yourself to the priest, and offer the gifts Moses prescribed for your purification as a testimony for them.'

But the man went out and started spreading the news of his cure, so Jesus could no longer go openly into any town; he withdrew instead to deserted places to pray. But large crowds came from every direction and followed him to hear him speak, and to be healed of diseases.

(MATTHEW 8:2–4; MARK 1:40–45; LUKE 5:12–16)

A PARALYSED MAN WALKS

esus got into a boat and crossed over to Capernaum, his own city. After a few days people heard he was back.

One day when he was teaching and preaching, Pharisees and teachers of the law were sitting before him from every village of Galilee and Judaea and from Jerusalem – so many that no more could get through the door.

The power of the Lord was in him to cure. Four men came carrying a paralysed man lying on a mattress; they had hoped to lay him in front of Jesus, but could not get in because of the crowd. So they went up on to the roof and made an opening in the tiles above him, and lowered the mattress on which the paralysed man was lying into the middle of the crowd in front of Jesus.

Seeing their faith, he said to the paralytic: 'Have courage, son; your sins are forgiven you.'

Some of the scribes and the Pharisees objected inwardly, and began saying to each other: 'Who is this man, and why does he talk blasphemy? Who but God can forgive sins?'

Jesus, knowing in himself that they were reasoning this way, said to them: 'Why do you think such evil things in your hearts? Which is easier to say to this paralysed man: "Your sins are forgiven," or: "Get up, pick up your mattress and walk"?

'But to prove to you that the Son of Man has authority on earth to forgive sins' – he said to the paralysed man – 'I tell you, stand up, pick up your mattress and go home.' At once the man stood up in front of them all, picked up his mattress, went out and walked home, praising God.

When the crowd saw this, they were astonished, bewildered and afraid; but they praised God, the only one who gives such power to men, and said: 'We have seen wonderful things today. We have never seen anything like this.'

(MATTHEW 9:1–8; MARK 2:1–12; LUKE 5:17–26)

THE CALLING OF MATTHEW

Jesus went out, but the crowd came to him beside the sea, so he taught them there. Then, walking on, he saw a tax collector named Matthew or Levi, the son of Alphaeus, sitting at the customs house. Jesus said to him, 'Follow me,' and leaving everything Levi got up and followed him.

Later he gave a big dinner for Jesus in his house, and many tax collectors and sinners came and reclined at table with him and his disciples; they were also his followers. When the Pharisees and their scribes saw this, they complained to the disciples: 'Why do you and your teacher eat and drink with tax collectors and sinners?'

Jesus heard this and answered them: 'It is not healthy people who need a doctor, but those who are sick. Go and learn what this means: I desire mercy, not sacrifice. Because I did not come to call righteous people, but sinners to repentance.'

(MATTHEW 9:9–13; MARK 2:13–17; LUKE 5:27–32)

WHY THE DISCIPLES OF JESUS DIDN'T FAST

When the disciples of John and those of the Pharisees were fasting, John's disciples came to Jesus and asked: 'Why is it that we and the Pharisees often fast and pray while your disciples go on eating and drinking?'

Jesus answered: 'Would you make wedding guests fast and mourn while the bridegroom was with them? They can't do that; they will fast later, when the bridegroom is taken away from them.'

He also told them a parable. 'No one tears a piece of cloth from a new cloak to patch an old one; it would spoil the new cloak and wouldn't match the old. Besides, the new cloth would pull away from the old, and make the tear worse.

'Nor does anyone put new wine into old wineskins; it would only burst them, and he would lose the wine and the skins. People put new wine into fresh skins, and both are preserved.

'But no one who has tasted old wine wants new; he says the old is good!'

(MATTHEW 9:14–17; MARK 2:18–22; LUKE 5:33–9)

JESUS IS MASTER OF THE SABBATH

esus was walking through the cornfields on a sabbath when his disciples felt hungry and began to pick ears of corn and rub them with their hands and eat them.

When some of the Pharisees saw this, they said to Jesus: 'Look, why are your disciples doing what is not lawful on a sabbath?'

Jesus answered: 'Have you never read what David did when he and his men were hungry: how he went into the house of God in the days of the high priest Abiathar and took the sacred loaves, and ate and gave them to those who were with him – bread which the law did not allow them to eat, but only the priests?

'And haven't you read in the law that the priests in the temple profane the sabbath and are guiltless? But I tell you, something greater than the temple is here.

'The sabbath was made for man, not man for the sabbath; so the Son of Man is Lord even of the sabbath. And you would not have condemned the guiltless if you had understood what this means: I desire mercy, not sacrifice.'

(MATTHEW 12:1–8; MARK 2:23–8; LUKE 6:1–5)

A MIRACLE ON THE SABBATH: THE MAN WITH THE WITHERED HAND

L eaving that place, he went into the synagogue on another sabbath and taught; and a man was there who had a withered right hand. The scribes and Pharisees asked Jesus whether it was lawful to heal on the sabbath, and observed him carefully to see what he would do. They were looking for something of which to accuse him.

Knowing what was in their minds, Jesus said: 'If one of you owns a sheep and it falls into a ditch on the sabbath, will he not lift it out? And isn't a man worth much more than a sheep? So it is lawful to do good on the sabbath.'

Then he said to the man with the withered hand: 'Stand up here in the middle,' and he did. Jesus said to the others: 'I ask you again: is it lawful to do good on the sabbath, or to do evil: to save life, or destroy it?' But they were silent.

Looking round at them angrily, grieved by their hardness of heart, he said to the man: 'Stretch out your hand.' He did so and it was healed, as healthy as the other.

Infuriated, the Pharisees walked out at once together with the Herodians, and took counsel with them about Jesus; they discussed what they could do to destroy him. Knowing this, Jesus left that place.

(MATTHEW 12:9–15A; MARK 3:1–6; LUKE 6:6–11)

JESUS CHOOSES THE TWELVE APOSTLES

esus then went up into the mountain and spent a whole
night praying. When it was day, he sent for the twelve disciples he had chosen to remain with him till he would send
them out to preach. They came to him and he gave them
authority to expel evil spirits, and to heal every sickness and
disease. He called them 'apostles'.

These are the names of the twelve apostles: first, Simon to
whom he gave the new name Peter, and Andrew his brother;
James the son of Zebedee and his brother John – Jesus gave
them the name Boanerges, 'sons of thunder'; Philip,
Bartholomew, Thomas, and Matthew the tax collector; James
the son of Alphaeus; Simon the Cananaean, also called the
Zealot; Jude or Thaddaeus, the brother of James, and Judas
Iscariot, the man who would betray him.

(MATTHEW 10:1–4; MARK 3:13–19; LUKE 6:12–16)

A TORRENT OF MIRACLES

esus went down to a level place on the coast with a large
number of his disciples. Great crowds of people who had
heard of the things he did had come to him from Galilee and
Decapolis, from Jerusalem and all Judaea, from Idumaea and
beyond the Jordan and from the coastal region around Tyre
and Sidon. News of him had even spread through Syria.

They came to listen to him and to be cured of their diseases.
They brought him the paralysed, people in pain or suffering

from different diseases, as well as the demon-possessed and the insane, and he healed them all.

The sick crowded around him trying to touch him, because power went out from him that cured them. He told his disciples to keep a boat near him in case the crowd threatened to crush him.

When the evil spirits saw him they fell down before him, crying out: 'You are the Son of God,' though he had strictly ordered them not to reveal who he was.

In this way what had been foretold through the prophet Isaiah was fulfilled:

'See my servant, whom I chose; my beloved, in whom my soul was well pleased. I will put my Spirit in him, and he will announce judgement to the nations. He will not bully or shout, nor will anyone hear his voice in the streets; he will not break the bruised reed, nor quench the smoking flax. He will lead justice to victory, and the gentiles will hope in his name.'

(MATTHEW 4:24–5; 12:15B–21; MARK 3:7–12; LUKE 6:17–19)

THE SERMON ON THE MOUNT

The Beatitudes

Seeing the crowds, he went up into the mountain. When he sat, his disciples came to him. Looking up, he began to speak; this is what he taught them:

'Blessed are the poor in spirit; the kingdom of heaven belongs to them.

'Blessed are those who mourn and weep now, because they will laugh and be comforted.

'Blessed are the gentle; they will inherit the earth.

'Blessed are those who now hunger and thirst for righteousness; they will be satisfied.

'Blessed are the merciful; they will receive mercy.

'Blessed are the pure in heart; they will see God.

'Blessed are the peacemakers; they will be called sons of God.

'Blessed are those who have been persecuted for doing what is right; the kingdom of heaven belongs to them.

'Blessed are you when men hate you on account of the Son of Man: when they reject and revile and persecute you, blacken your name and falsely accuse you of all kinds of evil. Rejoice when that happens, be glad and jump for joy; your reward will be great in heaven, because this is how their fathers persecuted the prophets before you.

'But woe to you who are rich, because you have your consolation now.

'Woe to you who are well filled now; you will go hungry.

'Woe to you who are laughing now; you will mourn and lament.

'Woe to you when all men speak well of you, because this is how their fathers spoke of the false prophets.

'You are the salt of the earth, and salt is good. But if it loses its saltiness, what can make it salty again? Then it is good for nothing, neither for the soil nor for the manure heap; it can only be thrown out and trodden on.

'You are the light of the world. A city set on a mountain cannot be hidden. People don't light a lamp and hide it under a bushel measure; they put it on a lampstand so that all who come in can see it, and it gives light to everyone in the house.

'Let your light shine for others in the same way, so that they see your good works and give glory to your Father in heaven.'

(MATTHEW 5:1–16; LUKE 6:12–19; 11:33;

14:34–5)

The Moral Laws of Moses Still Stand

'Do not think that I have come to cancel the law or the prophets; I have come not to cancel but to fulfil them. I assure you that till heaven and earth pass away, not one letter or tail of a letter of the law will be taken away until everything is fulfilled.

'So whoever breaks one of the least of these command-ments and teaches others to break it will be called least in the kingdom of heaven. The one who keeps and teaches them will be called great.

'But unless your righteousness exceeds that of the scribes and Pharisees, you will never get into the kingdom of heaven.'

(MATTHEW 5:17–20)

The Law of the Gospel: No Anger or Insults

'You have heard that the people of ancient times were told: "You must not commit murder, and everyone who murders must submit to the sentence of the court." But I tell you that whoever is angry with his brother will be liable to sen-tence. Whoever calls his brother an idiot will be liable to the

judgement of the sanhedrin, and whoever calls anyone a rene-
gade will be punished in the fire of hell.

'If while you bring your gift to the altar you remember that
your brother has anything against you, leave your gift there in
front of the altar; go first and be reconciled with your brother,
and then come and offer your gift.

'Try to satisfy your enemy while you are with him on the
way to court, so that he will not hand you over to the judge, and
the judge to the officer to put you in prison. I tell you, you will
certainly not be let out until you have repaid the last penny.'

(MATTHEW 5:21–6; LUKE 12:58–9)

Remove the Causes of Adultery

'You have heard that it was said: "You shall not commit adultery." But I tell you that whoever looks at a woman to desire
her has already committed adultery with her in his heart.

'So if your right eye causes you to sin, pluck it out and
throw it away; it is better for you if only one part of your body
is thrown on the fire and not the whole of it. And if your right
hand causes you to sin, cut it off and throw it away; it is better for you that one part of your body should perish than that
the whole of you should go into the fire.'

(MATTHEW 5:27–30)

No Remarriage After Divorce

'It was also said: "If anyone sends his wife away, let him give
her a bill of divorce." But I tell you that whoever divorces his
wife – not someone he fornicates with – and marries another
commits adultery; and a man who sends away his wife causes

her to commit adultery, because whoever marries a woman
divorced by her husband commits adultery.'

(MATTHEW 5:31–2; LUKE 16:18)

Tell the Truth and You Won't Need Oaths
'Again, you have heard that the people of ancient times were
told: "You must not swear an oath falsely, but must keep your
promises to the Lord."

'But I tell you not to swear at all: not by heaven, because it
is the throne of God; nor by the earth, because it is his footrest;
nor by Jerusalem, because it is the city of the great King; nor by
your head, because you cannot make one hair white or black.

'Just say yes when you mean yes, and no when you mean
no. Anything that goes beyond that is evil.'

(MATTHEW 5:33–7)

Don't Return Evil for Evil
'You have heard that it was said: "An eye for an eye, and a tooth
for a tooth."

'But I tell you not to oppose evil with evil. If someone slaps
your right cheek, offer him the other as well. If someone wants
to take you to court for your tunic, let him have your cloak too;
or if he takes your cloak, let him have your tunic. If someone
makes you walk a mile with him, go two miles.

'Give to everyone who asks of you. Don't turn away the one
who wants to borrow from you, and don't ask one who takes
your things to give them back.'

(MATTHEW 5:38–42; LUKE 6:29–30)

Love Even Your Enemies

'You have heard that it was said: "You must love your neighbour and hate your enemy."

'But this is what I tell you: love your enemies; do good to those who hate you, bless those who curse you and pray for those who insult you and persecute you. This will make you true children of your Father in heaven, because he makes his sun rise on evil men as well as good, and his rain fall on the righteous and unrighteous alike. He is kind to those who are evil and ungrateful, so you must show compassion as he does.

'To greet only your brothers and love only those who love you is no more than everyone does, so what reward or thanks would you deserve? Even tax collectors and sinners do that much. And if you lend to those from whom you expect to get interest, what thanks do you deserve? Sinners lend to sinners, even to get back the same amount.

'So do good and lend without regret, and your reward will be great; you will be children of the Most High. Be perfect as your heavenly Father is perfect.'

(MATTHEW 5:43–8; LUKE 6:27–8; 32–6)

Give Secretly to the Needy

'Make sure you don't do your good deeds in the sight of others to impress them, or you will have no reward from your Father in heaven.

'When you give to the needy, don't sound a trumpet before you, as hypocrites do in the synagogues and streets to get glory from others; I tell you truly, they have had their reward.

'Don't let your left hand know what your right hand is doing. Keep your giving secret, and your Father who sees every hidden thing will repay you.'

(MATTHEW 6:1–4)

Don't Pray for Show, and Be Brief

'When you pray, don't be like the hypocrites; they love to stand and pray in the synagogues and on street corners so as to be seen by others. I tell you truly, they have had their reward. When you pray, go into your private room, shut the door and pray to your Father secretly, and your Father who sees what is done in secret will repay you.

'And when you pray, do not use empty words as the gentiles do. They think they will only be heard if they make a long speech; don't be like them, because God your Father knows what you need before you ask him.'

Once when he had finished praying in a certain place, one of his disciples said: 'Lord, teach us to pray, just as John taught his disciples.' So he said to them: 'Pray like this:

Our Father in heaven, may your name be held holy.
May your kingdom come, and your will be done on earth as
    it is in heaven.
Give us enough bread for each day.
Forgive us our sins, as we have forgiven those who sinned
    against us.
Do not expose us to temptation, but rescue us from evil.

'When you stand praying, forgive anything you have against anyone. If you forgive men the wrong they do, your Father in heaven will forgive you your trespasses too; but if you do not forgive others, your Father will not forgive your wrongdoing.'

(MATTHEW 6:5–15; LUKE 11:1–4)

Persistence in Prayer

He said to them: 'Suppose you visit a friend at midnight and say to him: "Friend, lend me three loaves; another friend has stopped by on a journey, and I have nothing to offer him." And suppose he answers from inside the house: "Don't bother me; the door is shut, and my children and I are in bed; I can't get up now to give you bread."

'I tell you, even if he won't get up and give it to you just because he is your friend, he will do it if you persist in asking him, and will give you as much as you need.'

(LUKE 11:5–8)

Don't Make a Show of Fasting

'When you fast, don't put on show of gloom as the hypocrites do. They disfigure their faces so that people can see they are fasting; I tell you truly, they have had their reward. When you fast, dress your hair and wash your face so that people cannot see you are fasting, but only your Father who sees what is done secretly; then he will repay you.'

(MATTHEW 6:16–18)

Let Your Wealth Be in Heaven, Not on Earth

'Do not be afraid, little flock, because it has pleased your Father to give you the kingdom. So do not store up treasures for yourself on earth, where moth and rust spoil them and thieves break in and steal them. Sell your possessions and give to the poor; make yourselves purses that do not wear out. Store unfailing treasures for yourself in heaven, where no thief comes and no moth or rust destroys them; because where your treasure is, there will your heart be also.

'No one can serve two masters; either he will hate the one and love the other, or be loyal to one and despise the other. You cannot serve God and mammon.'

(MATTHEW 6:19–21,24; LUKE 12:32–4; 16:13)

Trust in God's Providence

Jesus said to his disciples: 'I tell you, do not be anxious about your life, about what you will eat or drink, or how you will clothe your body. Surely life is more than food, and the body more than clothes?

'Look at the ravens. Birds don't sow or reap or store produce in barns, yet your Father in heaven feeds them. Surely you are worth more than they are? And which of you, however he tries, can lengthen his life by one cubit? If you can't do that, why worry about these other things?

'Why worry about clothes? Consider the lilies of the field, and how they grow. They don't work; they don't spin or weave, yet I tell you, not even Solomon in all his glory was dressed as beautifully as they are. If God so dresses the plants that grow in the field today and are thrown into the oven tomorrow, how much more will he not clothe you, men of little faith?

'So don't be like the pagans, preoccupied with these things. Don't keep asking: "What shall we eat, what shall we drink, what shall we wear?" Your Father in heaven knows you need all these things; but look first for his kingdom and his righteousness, and then they will also be given to you.

'And don't worry about tomorrow; tomorrow will take care of itself. Every day has enough trouble of its own.'

(MATTHEW 6:25–34; LUKE 12:22–31)

Physical and Spiritual Blindness[3]

'The light of the body is the eye. If your eyes are healthy, the whole of you is in the light; but if something is wrong with them, you are in the dark.

'What matters most is never to let your inner light turn to darkness. What a darkness that is!

'When you are wholly enlightened, no part of you in darkness, then everything will be as clear to you as a shining light.'

(MATTHEW 6:22–3; LUKE 11:34–6)

Forgive, Don't Judge

'If you do not want to be judged, do not judge others; otherwise you will be judged in the same way. Do not condemn, and you will not be condemned.

'Forgive, and you will be forgiven. Give, and good things will be given to you in generous measure, shaken together, pressed down, running over and poured into your lap. The measure in which you give will be the measure in which you receive.'

Speaking in parables, he also said: 'Can one blind man guide another? Won't they both fall into a ditch?

'A student is not superior to his teacher; but when he has finished his studies, he will be like his teacher.

'Why do you see the speck in your brother's eye, but not the beam in your own? How can you say: "Brother, let me take the speck out of your eye," and not see the beam in your own? Hypocrite! First take the beam out of your eye, and then you'll see clearly enough to take the speck out of your brother's eye.'

(MATTHEW 7:1–5; LUKE 6:37–42)

Holy Things to the Holy

'Do not give what is holy to dogs or throw your pearls in front of pigs, or they may trample on them and then turn on you and bite you.'

(MATTHEW 7:6)

Whatever We Ask for, God Gives What Is Best

'Ask, I tell you, and you will receive; search and you will find; knock, and the door will be opened to you. Everyone who asks receives, everyone who searches finds, and the door will be opened to everyone who knocks.

'But what father among you would give his son a stone when he asked for a loaf, or give him a serpent instead of a fish, or a scorpion when he asked for an egg? If you, evil as you are, know how to give good gifts to your children, how much more will your Father in heaven give the Holy Spirit and all good things to those who ask him.'

(MATTHEW 7:7–11; LUKE 11:9–13)

The Golden Rule

'This is what the law and the prophets teach us: whatever you want people to do to you, do the same to them.'

(MATTHEW 7:12; LUKE 6:31)

Choose the Narrow Road

'Few people find the narrow gate and the path that leads to life; many go through the wide gate and take the broad road that leads to destruction. Do all you can to get in through the narrow gate, because I tell you, many will try and will not be able to.'

(MATTHEW 7:13–14; LUKE 13:24)

How to Tell Who Truly Speaks for God

'Beware of false prophets who come to you disguised as sheep, but are really greedy wolves. You will know them by their fruits, as you know a tree by its fruit; you don't pick grapes or figs from a thistle or a thorn bush.

'In the same way, a good tree bears good fruit; it cannot produce bad. But a corrupt tree bears bad fruit, and cannot produce good. And a tree that doesn't produce good fruit is cut down and thrown on the fire.

'A good person brings good things out of the treasure of goodness in his heart, but an evil person evil things out of the evil in his heart. His mouth utters the things that fill his heart.'

(MATTHEW 7:15–20; LUKE 6:43–5)

Obedience Gets Us into God's Kingdom: Mere Declarations Don't

'Why do you call me "Lord, Lord," and do not do what I say? Not everyone who calls me "Lord" will enter the kingdom of heaven; only the one who does the will of my Father in heaven.

'On the day that is coming, many will say to me: "Lord, Lord, didn't we prophesy in your name, and expel demons in your name, and do many deeds of power in your name?" But I will tell them: "I never knew you; leave me, all who break God's laws."'

(MATTHEW 7:21–3; LUKE 6:46)

Listen to What Jesus Says, and Do it

'I will show you what someone is like who comes to me and listens to my words and does what I say.

'He is like a prudent man building his house, who dug deep and laid a foundation on rock. When the rain came down and the wind blew and the rivers flooded and dashed against that house, they could not shake it; it did not fall, because it was solidly built, founded on rock.

'But anyone who hears these words of mine and does not act on them is like the fool who built his house on soil, without a foundation. So the rain came down and the river rose and the winds blew and beat against that house, and all at once it collapsed and was ruined.'

When Jesus had finished saying these things in their hearing, crowds of people followed him down the mountain and into Capernaum.

(MATTHEW 7:24–8A; 8:1; LUKE 6:47–9; 7:1)

THE CENTURION AND HIS SERVANT: 'LORD, I AM NOT WORTHY'

hen Jesus came into Capernaum, a certain centurion had a sick servant who was dear to him and near to death. Hearing about Jesus, he sent elders of the Jews[4] to beg of him: 'Lord, my servant has been put to bed in the house, paralysed and in great pain.'

Earnestly they asked Jesus to come and heal the servant. They said: 'He deserves that you should grant this, because he loves our nation, and built the synagogue for us.' Jesus answered: 'I will come and heal him', and went with them.

But when he was not far from the house, the centurion sent friends to say: 'Lord, do not trouble yourself. I am not worthy that you should come under my roof; that is why I did not count myself worthy to come to you.

'Just say the word, and my servant will be healed. I am under authority, and I have soldiers under me. I tell this one go, and he goes; another, come, and he comes; I tell my slave do this, and he does it.'

Hearing these words, Jesus marvelled; he turned to the crowd who were following him and said: 'I tell you truly, I have not found such faith in anyone in Israel. And indeed, many will come from east and west to recline at table with Abraham and Isaac and Jacob in the kingdom of heaven, while sons of the kingdom will be thrown out into the dark where there will be weeping and gnashing of teeth.'

Then he gave his answer: 'As you believe, let it be done for you.' And when those the centurion had sent came back to the house, they found the slave well again; he had been healed at that very hour.

(MATTHEW 8:5–13; LUKE 7:2–10)

A WIDOW'S ONLY SON BROUGHT BACK FROM DEATH

he next day Jesus went with his disciples and a large crowd into a town called Nain. As he came near to the gate of the town, a dead man was being carried out for burial, his mother's only son, and she was a widow. Quite a crowd of people of the town were with her.

When the Lord saw her, he felt compassion for her and said: 'Do not weep.' He went to the bier and touched it, and the bearers stood still. Then he said: 'Young man, I tell you, get up'; and the dead man sat up and began to speak, and Jesus gave him to his mother.

Fear gripped everyone, and they gave glory to God. They said: 'A great prophet has been raised up among us; God has visited his people!' And news of Jesus spread through all Judaea and the adjacent regions.

(LUKE 7:11–17)

DISCIPLES OF JOHN THE BAPTIST CONVINCED THAT JESUS IS THE MESSIAH

ohn's disciples reported to him in prison all these deeds of Christ. John then summoned two of them and sent them to the Lord to ask whether he was the one to come, or whether they should expect someone else.

So they came to Jesus and said: 'John the Baptist sent us to ask you: are you the one who is to come, or should we wait for someone else?'

Just then Jesus had healed many people of diseases and plagues and evil spirits, and restored the sight of many who had been blind. So he answered them: 'Go and report to John what you have seen and heard: the blind see again, the lame walk, the deaf hear, lepers are healed, the dead are brought back to life, and poor people hear the good news.

'Blessed is the one who does not find me a stumbling-block.'

(MATTHEW 11:2–6; LUKE 7:18–23)

JESUS CALLS JOHN THE GREATEST MAN BEFORE HIM

s these messengers of John were leaving, Jesus began to speak about John to the crowds.

'What did you go into the desert to see? A reed shaken by the wind? No. What then? A man dressed in soft clothes? But those who wear fine clothes and live in luxury are in the palaces of kings. So why did you go out? What did you go to see?

'A prophet? Yes, I tell you, and more than a prophet. This is the one about whom it was written: "See, I send my messenger ahead of you to prepare your way before you."

'I tell you truly, among all those born of women there has not arisen a greater man than John the Baptist – though the least in the kingdom of God is greater than he.

'The law and all the prophets spoke of John. And since the day he began to preach about the kingdom of God, everyone is pressing to get into it, and the violent are trying to take it by force.

'If you are ready to accept this, John is Elijah, the one who was to come. He who has ears, let him listen!

'Those who listened to John, even tax collectors, acknowledged God's justice by receiving his baptism. But the Pharisees and the lawyers, by refusing it, refused what God asked of them.

'So to what shall I compare the people of this generation: what are they like? They are like children sitting in the marketplace, complaining to the others: "We played the pipes for you, and you wouldn't dance; we sang mourning songs, and you wouldn't cry."

'John the Baptist came, not eating bread nor drinking wine, and they say he has a demon. The Son of Man came eating and drinking, and they say: Look, a glutton and a wine drinker, a friend of tax collectors and sinners.

'But to her children, wisdom is justified in everything she does.'

(MATTHEW 11:7–19; LUKE 7:24–35; 16:16)

A REPENTANT SINNER ANOINTS THE FEET OF JESUS

A certain Pharisee invited Jesus to a meal, so he went into the house and reclined at table. A woman of the town who was a sinner knew that he was there. She brought an alabaster box of ointment and stood behind him at his feet. Weeping, she began to wet his feet with her tears and wipe them with her hair; then she kissed them fervently, and anointed them with the ointment.

The Pharisee who had invited Jesus saw this and thought to himself: 'If this man were a prophet, he would have known who and what sort of woman was touching him.'

Jesus responded: 'Simon, I have something to say to you.' Simon answered: 'Teacher, say it.'

'A certain creditor had two debtors; one owed him five hundred denarii and the other fifty. Since they had no means of repaying, he freely forgave both. Which of them will love him more?'

Simon answered: 'I suppose the one to whom he forgave the more.' Jesus said to him: 'You judge rightly.'

Then, turning to the woman, he said to Simon: 'You see this woman? I came into your house, and you gave me no water for my feet; but this woman has wet my feet with tears, and wiped them with her hair. You gave me no kiss, but this woman has not stopped kissing my feet. You did not anoint my head with oil, but this woman has anointed my feet with ointment.

'I tell you that since she has loved so much, many sins must have been forgiven her. It's the one to whom little is forgiven that has little love.'

Then he said to the woman: 'Your sins are forgiven.' And those reclining with him began to ask each other: Who is this, who even forgives sins? But Jesus said to her: 'Your faith has saved you, go in peace.'

(LUKE 7:36–50)

WOMEN PROVIDE FOR JESUS AND THE TWELVE

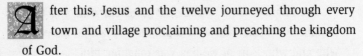 fter this, Jesus and the twelve journeyed through every town and village proclaiming and preaching the kingdom of God.

With them were certain women who had been healed of evil spirits and illnesses: Mary called Magdalene, from whom seven demons had gone out, and Joanna the wife of Herod's steward Chuza, and Susanna, and many others who supplied their needs out of their own possessions.

(LUKE 8:1–3)

THE RELATIVES OF JESUS AND HIS SPIRITUAL FAMILY

esus went into a house, but again such a crowd gathered that he and the twelve could not even eat. When his mother and his relatives heard this, they came to take charge of him, because they said: 'He is beside himself.' But they could not get near him while he was still speaking to the crowd that sat around him.

Standing outside and wanting to speak to him, they sent in a message calling him, and one of the crowd passed it on: 'Your mother and your brothers are standing outside; they want to see you and talk to you.'

But Jesus answered: 'Who is my mother, and who are my brothers?' Looking at the circle around him, he stretched out his hand to his disciples and said: 'See, these are my mother and my brothers. Whoever hears the word and does the will of God my Father in heaven is my brother and sister and mother.'

(MATTHEW 12:46–50; MARK 3:20–21,31–5;
LUKE 8:19–21)

THE PARABLE OF THE SOWER AND THE SEED

n a day when a great crowd of people from every town came to him, Jesus again left the house and taught beside the sea. He sat in a boat offshore while the crowd stood on the beach, and he told them many things in parables like this one:

'Listen, all of you. A farmer went out to sow seed. As he sowed, some of the seed fell on the path, and was trodden on, and birds came and ate it.

'Some of the seed fell on stony ground where there was not much earth, so it sprang up too soon, without root or moisture. When the sun rose it was scorched and withered.

'Some seed fell among thorns which grew with it and choked it, so that it did not bear fruit.

'But some fell into good earth and flourished, producing thirty, sixty or a hundredfold.'

He said this and called out: 'Whoever has ears, let him hear!'

Later, when he was alone, the twelve and those around him came to question him about this and other parables. They asked him: 'Why do you speak to them in parables?'

He answered: 'Because to you it has been granted to know the mysteries of the kingdom of God, but not to the others. To those outside, I tell everything in parables, because when they see they do not perceive, and when they hear they do not understand, for fear of changing their ways and being forgiven. In them Isaiah's prophecy is fulfilled:

"You will listen and hear, but not understand; you will look and see, but not perceive. Because the mind of this people has grown dull; they have blocked their ears and closed their eyes, so as not to see with their eyes and hear with their ears and understand with their hearts, and turn back and be healed by me."'

Then he said to them: 'Don't you understand this parable of the sower? Then how will you understand the others?

'This is what the parable means: the seed the man sows is God's message. The path on which some of it falls stands for people who hear the news of the kingdom but do not understand it. When that happens, Satan the evil one comes at once and plucks away what was sown in their hearts, so that they will not believe and be saved.

'The stony ground stands for those who accept the message with joy as soon as they hear it, but have no root in themselves; they don't last. They believe for a while, but in time of trial, or as soon as believers are persecuted, their faith is brought down and they fall away.

'Those who receive the seed among thorns hear the message, but the anxiety and worries of the time and the traps of wealth and lust for pleasure come in and choke the message so that it bears no fruit in them.

'The good earth is those who hear and understand the message and welcome it into a good and receptive heart: those who hold fast to it in patience and produce its fruit, thirty, sixty or a hundredfold.'

(MATTHEW 13:1–11,13–15,18–23; MARK 4:1–20;
LUKE 8:4–15)

JESUS REVEALS THE MYSTERIES OF THE KINGDOM

Jesus said to them: 'No one who has lit a lamp hides it in a jar or puts it under the couch or the bushel measure. He puts it on the lampstand, so that all who come in can see its light.

'There is nothing hidden that will not be revealed, and nothing kept secret which will not inevitably come into the open and be known; if anyone has ears to hear, let him pay attention to this.'

And he said: 'What is given to you will be measured out with the same measure you use. So whoever has something will receive more; but from him who has nothing, even what he seems to have will be taken from him.'

(MATTHEW 13:12; MARK 4:21–5; LUKE 8:16–18)

The Kingdom Grows Like a Seed

Jesus said: 'The kingdom of God is like this: a man throws seed on the earth, and sleeps and gets up night and day; and the seed sprouts and grows, he doesn't know how. Of its own accord the earth bears fruit: first the stalk, then the ear, then the full corn in the ear. And when it is ready he gets out his sickle at once, because the harvest has come.'

(MARK 4:26–9)

The Enemy Plants Traitors among the Citizens of the Kingdom

Jesus put before them another parable: 'The kingdom of heaven is like this. A householder sowed good seed in his field, but while his men were sleeping, his enemy came and sowed weeds among the wheat and went away.

'So when the wheat sprouted and produced its grain, the weeds appeared too. The householder's servants came to him and said: "Lord, surely you sowed good seed in your field; where did the weeds come from?" He answered: "An enemy has done this."

'So the servants asked: "Do you want us then to go and pull them up?" But he said: "No, because when you pull up the weeds you may pull up the wheat as well. Leave both to grow till the harvest, and then I will tell the reapers: 'First collect the weeds, and bind them in bundles to burn; then gather the wheat into my barn.'"'

Then, sending away the crowds, Jesus came into the house, and his disciples came to him and said: 'Explain to us the parable of the weeds of the field.'

68

He answered: 'The one sowing the good seed is the Son of Man, and the field is the world. The good seed is the sons of the kingdom, and the weeds are the sons of the evil one. The enemy who sows them is the devil; the harvest is the end of the world, and the reapers are angels.

'The weeds are collected and burned, and that is how it will be at the end of the world. The Son of Man will send his angels and they will collect from his kingdom all who break God's laws and lead others to sin, and will throw them into the furnace where there will be wailing and gnashing of teeth. Then the righteous will shine like the sun in the kingdom of their Father.

'Whoever has ears, let him listen.'

(MATTHEW 13:24–30,36–43)

Small Beginning, Great Fulfilment

He introduced another parable by saying: 'To what can I compare the kingdom of God? What parable will describe it?

'The kingdom of heaven is like the mustard seed which a man took and sowed on his ground. When it is sown in the ground, it is smaller than other seeds, but when it comes up it grows taller than all the grasses and becomes a tree, with branches big enough for birds to come and nest in, and to rest under its shade.' He also told them this parable: 'The kingdom of heaven is like yeast which a woman took and hid in three measures of flour, and soon all of it was leavened.'

(MATTHEW 13:31–3; MARK 4:30–32;
LUKE 13:18–20)

The Treasure and the Pearl

'The kingdom of heaven is like treasure which a man found hidden in a field, and hid again. With joy he went and sold all he had to buy that field.

'Again, the kingdom of heaven is like a merchant looking for beautiful pearls. Finding one specially valuable pearl, he goes and sells everything he has to buy it.'

(MATTHEW 13:44–6)

The Net Full of Fish Good and Bad

'Again, the kingdom of heaven is like a net thrown into the sea that gathers every kind of fish. When it is full, they drag it ashore, and sitting down they collect the good fish into baskets but throw out the bad ones.

'So it will be at the end of the world: the angels will go out and separate the evil men from among the righteous, and will throw them into the blazing furnace, where there will be wailing and gnashing of teeth.'

(MATTHEW 13:47–50)

Conclusion

Jesus revealed the truth to the crowds in parables like these, as many as they were able to hear, and told them nothing except in a parable; but to his disciples, he explained everything privately. In this way he fulfilled what the prophet said: 'I will open my mouth in parables, and utter things hidden since the foundation of the world.'

Then he asked the disciples: 'Have you understood all these things?' They said yes, so he added: 'Every scribe who becomes a disciple of the kingdom of heaven is like a householder who brings out of his treasure things new and old.'

(MATTHEW 13:34–5,51–2; MARK 4:33–4)

EVEN WIND AND SEA OBEY JESUS

When evening came and Jesus had finished telling these parables, he left that place. To escape from the crowd around him, he said: 'Let us cross over to the other side of the lake.'

His disciples took him into a boat just as he was. They put to sea with some other boats, and as they sailed he fell asleep.

Then a great storm of wind arose, and waves beat into the boat and began to fill it. They were in danger, but Jesus remained asleep on the cushion in the stern.

They went to wake him and said: 'Teacher, Lord, save us! Doesn't it matter to you that we are perishing?' He answered: 'Why are you so afraid? How is it you have so little faith?'

Then he got up and rebuked the wind and the raging water, saying: 'Peace! Be quiet.' The wind dropped, and there was a great calm.

The men marvelled and began to be much afraid. They said to one another: 'Who can this man be, and what kind of a man? He commands even the winds and the sea, and they obey him.'

(MATTHEW 13:53; 8:18,23–7; MARK 4:35–40;
LUKE 8:22–5)

THE STRANGE CASE OF THE GADARENE SWINE

They sailed down the other side of the lake opposite Galilee and came to the country of the Gerasenes or Gadarenes. As soon as Jesus got out of the boat, two men came to him who were possessed by demons.

One came from the town, but no longer lived in his house; he was driven by the demon into deserted places among the tombs, and for some time had worn no clothes. He was extremely dangerous, so that no one dared to pass that way.

The unclean spirit often seized him, and no one could subdue him any more. He had been put under guard and bound with fetters and chains, but had broken free of them many times. Night and day, among the tombs and in the mountains, he used to cry out and cut himself with stones.

Seeing Jesus from a distance, he ran and knelt before him. Jesus commanded: 'Unclean spirit, come out of the man.' It responded: 'I beg of you and adjure you by God not to torment me.'

Then both the possessed men cried out: 'Jesus, Son of God most High, what have you to do with us? Have you come here to torture us before the time?'

Jesus asked the first: 'What is your name?' Many demons had entered him, so he answered: 'My name is Legion, because we are many.'

The demons implored Jesus not to send them out of the country, or into the abyss. On a hill some distance away, a large herd of pigs was feeding, and they begged: 'If you turn us out, send us into those pigs.'

Jesus said: 'Go,' and coming out, the unclean spirits went into the pigs and the whole herd of about two thousand rushed down the slope into the lake and were drowned.

When the men who had been feeding the pigs saw this, they ran away and reported it in the town and the fields and on the farms, and everyone came out to see what had happened and to meet Jesus.

They found the man whom the legion of demons had left sitting at Jesus' feet, clothed and in his senses. Those who had witnessed it told them how the man was healed, and about the pigs.

They were seized with great fear and began to beseech him to leave the Gerasene territory, so he got into a boat and went back. As he embarked, the man who had been possessed by demons begged to go with him.

He would not let him, but sent him away, saying: 'Go back to your house and your own people and tell them how the Lord God took pity on you, and what he did for you.' So the man began to proclaim all over the town and throughout the Decapolis region what Jesus had done for him, and everyone marvelled.

(MATTHEW 8:28–34; MARK 5:1–20; LUKE 8:26–39)

THE RAISING OF THE DAUGHTER OF JAIRUS

When Jesus had crossed to the other side and returned to his own town, a great crowd was waiting on the shore to welcome him.

73

A leader of the synagogue named Jairus came up to him, knelt in homage and begged him to come to his house. He had an only daughter who was about 12 years old, and he said: 'My daughter is at the point of death, or already dead. Please come and lay your hands on her to heal her and let her live.' So Jesus got up and followed him with his disciples.

A great crowd accompanied them and were pressing against Jesus. Among them was a woman who had suffered for 12 years from a flow of blood. No one could heal her. She had endured many treatments by various doctors and spent all she had, but nothing helped – in fact she was worse.

She had heard many things about Jesus, so approaching him from behind she touched the fringe of his cloak, telling herself: 'If I can only touch even his cloak, I shall be healed.' At once the flow of blood dried up. She could feel that she was cured of her illness, and Jesus knew immediately that power had gone out from him. Turning to the crowd, he asked: 'Who touched my cloak?'

No one owned up, and Peter said: 'Master, you see the crowds jostling and pressing against you. How can you ask who touched you?'

But Jesus answered: 'Someone did touch me; I know that power went out of me,' and he looked round to see who had done it; he looked at the woman, and she saw she had been discovered.

Trembling and afraid, but knowing what had happened to her, she knelt before him and told him the truth in front of everyone: why she had touched him, and how she had instantly been cured.

He said to her: 'Daughter, your faith has healed you; go in peace, and be free of your illness.' And the woman was well from then on.

While he was still speaking, some people came from the house of the synagogue leader to tell him: 'Your daughter has died. There is no need now to trouble the teacher.' But when he heard this Jesus said to the leader of the synagogue: 'Don't be afraid; only believe, and she will be healed.'

When they came to his house, Jesus let no one go in with him except Peter, James and his brother John and the girl's father and mother. Hearing the flute players and the weeping and wailing of the crowd, he said to them: 'Why all this uproar? Stop crying; go away. The girl has not died, she's asleep.' They laughed at him because they knew she was dead, but he made the crowd go away.

Then Jesus took the child's parents and those who were with him and went in to where the child was. Taking hold of her hand, he said to her: *Talitha, koum* ('Little girl, get up').

Her spirit returned and the girl got up at once and walked, and Jesus told her parents to give her something to eat.

They were astonished. He ordered them strictly to tell no one what had happened; no one was supposed to know, but the news spread throughout the country.

(MATTHEW 9:1,18B–26A; MARK 5:21–43;
LUKE 8:40–56)

THE PHARISEES' THEORY: JESUS AN AGENT OF SATAN

As Jesus was leaving, two blind men followed him crying out: 'Son of David, have pity on us!' When he went into the house they came to him, and he asked them: 'Do you believe I can do this?' They said: 'Yes, Lord.'

Then he touched their eyes, saying: 'According to your faith, let it be done to you,' and their eyes were opened.

Jesus sternly admonished them, saying: 'See that you let no one know.' But they went out and spread the news of him in all that region.

Then people brought to Jesus a dumb man possessed by a demon; and when the demon was expelled, the dumb man spoke.

The crowds marvelled, saying: 'Never was anything like this seen in Israel.' But the Pharisees said: 'It is by the power of the ruler of the demons that he exorcizes them.'

(MATTHEW 9:27–34)

JESUS REJECTED AND THREATENED IN NAZARETH

Jesus left that place and returned to his home town, followed by his disciples. When sabbath came he began to teach in their synagogue. Many heard him and were astonished and said: 'Isn't this the son of Joseph the carpenter? Isn't his mother called Mary? Are not his brothers James and Joseph, or

Joses, and Simon and Judas? And his sisters, are they not all here with us?

'So where does the man get these things? What is this wisdom given to him, and these acts of power done through his hands?' He upset them.

But Jesus said to them: 'No doubt you will quote me the proverb: "Physician, heal yourself"; or tell me: "Do here in your home town the things we heard you did in Capernaum."

'I assure you, no prophet is accepted in his home town. The one place where he gets no honour is among his relatives and in his own house.

'After all there were many widows in Israel in Elijah's day, when no rain fell for three years and six months and the whole country suffered a great famine; but he was not sent to any of them, only to a widow at Zarephath in Sidon.

'And there were many lepers in Israel in the days of the prophet Elisha, but not one of them was healed; only Naaman the Syrian.'

When they heard this everyone in the synagogue was enraged. They got up and drove him out of the town to the brow of the hill it was built on, wanting to throw him down; but he passed through the midst of them and went away. Marvelling at their unbelief, he would not work miracles there, except to lay his hands on a few sick people and cure them.

(MATTHEW 13:54–8; MARK 6:1–6A;
LUKE 4:22B–30)

THE TWELVE SENT ON A MISSION

esus made a tour of the villages, teaching. The crowds filled him with compassion because they were confused and demoralized, like sheep without a shepherd. Then he said to his disciples: 'The harvest is abundant but the workmen too few, so pray to the Lord of the harvest to send workers into his fields.'

He called the twelve together and prepared to send them out in pairs. He gave them authority and power to expel every kind of demon and heal every sickness, and instructed them as follows:

'Do not go among gentiles or into any Samaritan town; go rather to the lost sheep of the house of Israel. Wherever you go, proclaim that the kingdom of God has come close. Heal the sick, raise the dead, cure the lepers, expel demons. You have received freely; now give freely. Take nothing for your journey; do not carry silver, copper or brass in your belts or wallets, or a spare tunic or sandals or staff,[5] or bread, because the workman deserves to be given his food.

'Whatever town or village you go into, ask for a suitable person to lodge with and stay with that family till you leave. When you go into a house, bless it; if the family deserves it, your peace will come among them. If not, it will come back to you. If people refuse to have you or will not listen to you, leave that house or town and shake off the dust from under your feet as a testimony against them. I tell you truly, the land of Sodom and Gomorrah will bear the day of judgement more easily than such a town.

'See, I am sending you out like sheep among wolves; so be cunning as snakes, but harmless as doves.'

So they began their mission, exhorting people to repent of their sins. They expelled many demons; they anointed many who were sick with oil and healed them. When they came back they met together with Jesus and reported to him everything they had done and taught.

(MATTHEW 9:36–8; 10:1,5–L6; MARK 6:6B–13,30;
LUKE 9:1–6,10A)

HERODIAS GETS HER CHANCE TO HAVE JOHN THE BAPTIST KILLED

A suitable day came when King Herod gave a feast on his birthday for his courtiers and captains of a thousand and the chief men of Galilee. When the daughter of Herodias came in and danced among them, she pleased Herod and those reclining at table with him so much that he promised with an oath to give the girl whatever she wished. He swore to her: 'Whatever you ask I will give you, up to half of my kingdom.'

She went out and said to her mother: 'What should I ask for?' Herodias told her: 'The head of John, that man who baptizes.' So she hurried back and said to the king: 'I want you to give me the head of John the Baptist, here and now on a dish.'

This deeply grieved the king, but he did not want to refuse her because of the oaths he had made in front of those who were with him at table. So he sent an executioner at once, ordering him to bring John's head and give it to her. The executioner went and beheaded John in the prison, brought his head on a dish and gave it to the girl who gave it to her mother. When John's disciples heard this they went and took his body, laid it in a tomb and then came and reported it to Jesus.

(MATTHEW 14:6–12; MARK 6:21–9)

HEROD HEARS ABOUT JESUS: HAS JOHN COME BACK TO LIFE?

y this time Jesus had become widely known, and Herod the tetrarch heard reports about him and all that was happening. Some were saying that John the Baptist had been raised from death, and that this was why he could work miracles.

King Herod was perplexed. He said to his servants: 'John I beheaded, but who is this about whom I hear such things?'

Others said Jesus was Elijah who had reappeared, or another of the ancient prophets who had risen again. Hearing all these opinions, Herod decided: 'He is John whom I beheaded; he has been raised to life.' And he wanted to see Jesus.

(MATTHEW 14:1–2; MARK 6:14–16; LUKE 9:7–9)

THE FIRST MULTIPLICATION OF LOAVES AND FISHES

he Jewish feast of Passover was near, and so many people were coming and going that the disciples had no chance even to eat. So Jesus said: 'Come to a place where there are no people and rest a little.' Without telling anyone they went by boat over the sea of Galilee or Tiberias to a town called Bethsaida.

But many saw them going, and as the word spread a great crowd from all the towns followed Jesus on foot, because they had seen the miracles he worked for sick people. Running and walking, they reached Bethsaida before him.

As soon as he came ashore Jesus went up the mountain and sat there with his disciples. But when he looked up and saw the crowd coming, he was filled with compassion for them, because they were like sheep without a shepherd. He welcomed them and began to speak about the kingdom of God, and taught them many things. He also cured those who were sick and in need of healing.

When evening came, the twelve came to him and said: 'It is late now, and this is a lonely place. Send the crowd away, so that they can go to the villages and farms round about to find lodging and buy food.'

Jesus answered: 'You give them something to eat.' Then he asked Philip: 'Where can we buy bread for them?' This was only to test Philip; he knew what he was going to do.

Philip answered: 'Two hundred denarii wouldn't buy enough bread for everyone to have even a little.' And the disciples asked Jesus: 'Do you want us to go and buy it?'

He asked them: 'How much bread have you? Go and see.' One of the disciples, Andrew – Simon Peter's brother – said: 'There is a boy here who has five barley loaves and two fish; but what is that among so many?'

Jesus said: 'Bring them here to me.' Then he told his disciples: 'Make the people recline in groups of about fifty.' They did so;

there was plenty of green grass, and the people reclined in groups of fifty or a hundred. There were about five thousand men.

Jesus took the five loaves and the two fish, looked up to heaven, gave thanks and blessed them. Then he broke the loaves, and gave them to the disciples to distribute to the crowd, and divided the two fish among them all in the same way. They all ate as much as they wanted.

When they were satisfied, he said to his disciples: 'Collect the pieces left over so that nothing gets lost.' So they collected them and filled twelve baskets with the scraps left over by those who had eaten: five thousand men, not counting women and children.

Seeing the miracle Jesus had worked, the people said: 'This really is the prophet who was to come into the world.' But Jesus, knowing that they were about to take him and make him a king, went away again to the mountain alone.

(MATTHEW 14:13–21; MARK 6:31–44; LUKE
9:10B–17; JOHN 6:1–15)

JESUS WALKS ON THE LAKE

hen evening came, Jesus told his disciples to get into the boat and go ahead of him to the other side of Bethsaida while he sent the crowd away. When he had said goodbye to them, he went up into the mountain alone to pray.

The disciples went down to the shore. When it was already dark and Jesus still had not come to them, they put to sea and made for Capernaum.

Alone on the land when the boat was well out to sea, Jesus could see them struggling to row, because a strong wind blew against them and they were battling the waves. In the fourth watch of the night, early in the morning when they had rowed about three miles, they saw Jesus coming toward them walking on the sea. All the disciples saw him; he came near the boat as if he meant to pass by them.

They were troubled and cried out in fear, thinking he was a ghost. But at once he called out to them: 'Take courage, it's me; don't be afraid.'

Peter answered: 'Lord, if it is you, command me to come to you on the water'; and Jesus said: 'Come.' Getting down from the boat, Peter started walking on the water towards Jesus. But when he felt the wind he was afraid and began to sink, and cried out: 'Lord, save me.' Jesus stretched out his hand and took hold of him, and said: 'Man of little faith, why did you doubt?'

Then they wanted to take Jesus into the boat. As he got in the wind stopped, and in no time the boat was at the shore they were heading for. They were absolutely astonished, because they had not understood what the miracle of the loaves meant; their minds had been closed. Now they worshipped Jesus, saying: 'Truly, you are the Son of God.'

Going further, they anchored at Gennesaret. When they got out of the boat the people of that place recognized Jesus at once. They sent men running through all that region, and began bringing him all who were sick, carrying them on mattresses to wherever they heard he was. Whatever village, town or country place he visited, they put sick people in the marketplaces and begged him just to let them touch the fringe of his cloak; and all who touched it were healed.

(MATTHEW 14:22–36; MARK 6:45–56;
JOHN 6:16–21)

JESUS, THE BREAD OF LIFE

The next day the crowd that had stayed across the water realized that there was only one boat, and that Jesus had not got into the other one with his disciples, who had left without him. But other boats from Tiberias had come near the place where they had eaten the bread after the Lord gave thanks, so when they saw that neither Jesus nor his disciples were there, they got into those boats and came to Capernaum looking for Jesus. When they found him, they said: 'Rabbi, when did you come here?'

Jesus Calls for Faith in Himself
Jesus answered: 'I tell you truly, you are not looking for me because you saw miracles, but because you ate the loaves and were satisfied. Do not work for food that goes bad, but for food that keeps for eternal life which the Son of Man will give you, because he is the one on whom God the Father has set his seal.'

So they asked him: 'What kind of work does God want us to do?' Jesus answered: 'This is the work God wants of you, that you believe in the one he sent.'

Then they asked: 'What sign will you give us, so that we can see it and believe you? What miracle will you work? Our fathers ate the manna in the desert, as it is written: He gave them bread from heaven to eat.'

Jesus replied: 'Truly I tell you, it was not Moses who gave you bread from heaven; it is my Father who gives you the true bread from heaven, because the bread of God is the one who comes down from heaven and gives life to the world.'

So they said to him: 'Lord, give us this bread always.'

Jesus, the Living Bread from Heaven

Jesus said to them: 'I am the bread of life. Whoever comes to me will never hunger, and whoever believes in me will never thirst. But as I told you, even though you have seen me you do not believe.

'All those the Father gives me will come to me, and I will not turn one of them away, because I have come down from heaven not to do my own will but the will of the one who sent me. And his will is that I should not lose anyone he has given me, but that everyone who sees the Son and believes in him should have eternal life; and I will raise him up on the last day.'

Then the Jews complained about him because he said: 'I am the bread that has come down from heaven.' They said: 'Isn't this Jesus the son of Joseph? We know his father and mother. How can he now say: I have come down from heaven?'

Jesus answered: 'Do not complain among yourselves. No one can come to me unless the Father who sent me draws him, and he is the one I will raise up on the last day.

'It is written in the prophets: "They shall all be taught by God." Whoever listens to the Father and learns from him comes to me. Not that anyone has seen the Father except the one who comes from God; he has seen the Father.

'Truly I tell you, the one who believes has eternal life. I am the bread of life. Your fathers ate the manna in the desert and died; but this is the bread that comes down from heaven, so that whoever eats it does not die.

'I am the living bread that has come down from heaven. Whoever eats this bread will live for ever, and the bread which I will give for the life of the world is my own flesh.'

Jesus, the Food of Eternal Life

Now the Jews argued among themselves, saying: 'How can this man give us his flesh to eat?' But Jesus said to them: 'In all truth I tell you, unless you eat the flesh of the Son of Man and drink his blood, you do not have life in you. The one who eats my flesh and drinks my blood has eternal life, and I will raise him up at the last day.

'My flesh is real food, and my blood is real drink. Whoever eats my flesh and drinks my blood remains in me, and I in him. As the living Father sent me and I live because of the Father, so whoever eats me will live because of me.

'This is the bread that has come down from heaven: not like the bread the fathers ate, and died. Whoever eats this bread will live for ever.' He said these things in a synagogue while he was teaching in Capernaum.

Many of his disciples who heard him said: 'This is a hard teaching. Who could accept it?' But Jesus, knowing in himself that his disciples were complaining about it, said to them: 'Does this offend you? Then what if you see the Son of Man ascending to where he was before?

'The spirit is what gives life; the flesh yields nothing. The words I have spoken to you are spirit and life, but there are some of you who do not believe.' From the beginning, Jesus knew who they were that did not believe, and who it was that would betray him. So he said: 'This is why I told you that no one can come to me unless it is given to him by the Father.'

From then on, many of his disciples went home and no longer walked with him. So Jesus said to the twelve: 'Do you want to go away too?' Simon Peter answered him: 'Lord, who would we go to? You have the message of eternal life, and we have believed and known that you are the holy one of God.'

Jesus answered: 'Did I not choose the twelve of you? And one of you is a devil.' He meant Judas the son of Simon Iscariot, because this was the one who would betray him: one of the twelve.

(JOHN 6:22–72)

JESUS SPEAKS OF GOD AS HIS OWN FATHER

After this Jesus went up to Jerusalem for a Jewish feast. At the sheep gate in Jerusalem there is a pool with five porches, called Bethzatha in Hebrew. In the porches lay a crowd of sick people, the blind, the lame and the paralysed;[6] and there was a certain man there who had been ill for thirty-eight years.

Seeing this man and knowing how long he had lain there, Jesus said to him: 'Do you want to be made whole?' The invalid answered: 'Sir, I have no man to put me in the pool when the water is troubled. While I am getting in, someone gets in before me.'

Jesus said to him: 'Get up, pick up your mattress and walk.' And at once the man was healed, and took his mattress and walked.

That day was a sabbath, so the Jews said to him: 'Today is a sabbath; it is not lawful for you to carry that mattress.' But he answered them: 'The one who made me whole told me: Pick up your mattress and walk.'

They asked him: 'Who is the one that told you to pick up your mattress and walk?' But the man did not know who he was; Jesus had withdrawn because of the crowd in the place.

Later, Jesus found him in the temple and said: 'Look, you have been made whole; don't go on sinning, or something worse may happen to you.'

The man went away and told the Jews that Jesus was the one who had cured him, so they began to harass Jesus for doing such things on a sabbath. But he answered them: 'My Father works until now, and so do I.'

For this they wanted all the more to kill him: not only did he break the sabbath, but he spoke of God as his own Father, making himself equal to God.

(JOHN 5:1–18)

THE SON DOES ONLY WHAT HIS FATHER DOES

Jesus therefore answered them: 'Truly I tell you, the Son cannot do anything of himself, but only what he sees the Father doing. Whatever the Father does the Son does too, because the Father loves the Son and shows him everything he does.

'And he will show him greater deeds than these for you to marvel at, because as the Father raises the dead and gives life, so too the Son gives life to whoever he will.

'The Father judges no one, but has committed all judgement to the Son, so that everyone should honour the Son as they honour the Father. Whoever does not honour the Son does not honour the Father who sent him. But I assure you, whoever listens to my teaching and believes the one who sent me has eternal life. He does not receive condemnation, but has passed over from death into life.

'Truly I tell you, an hour is coming – in fact it is already here – when the dead will hear the voice of the Son of God, and those who listen will live. Just as the Father has life in himself, he has given the Son life in himself; and because the Son is man, he has given him authority to judge mankind.

'Do not be astonished by this: an hour is coming in which all who have died will hear his voice. Those who have done good will come out of their graves to a resurrection of life, while those who have done evil will come to a resurrection of judgement.

'I cannot do anything of myself; I judge according to what I hear. And my judgement is just, because I do not seek my own will, but the will of him who sent me.'

(JOHN 5:19–30)

THE FATHER BEARS WITNESS TO THE SON

'I f I testified about myself, my testimony would not be valid; but there is someone else who testifies on my behalf, and I know his testimony is true.

'You sent people to listen to John, and he testified to the truth. I do not need any man's testimony, but I say this for your sake, so that you may be saved.

'John was a burning, shining lamp, and for a time you were content to rejoice in his light; but the testimony I bear is greater than John's.

'The work the Father has given me to finish, the very miracles I do, prove that I am the one the Father has sent; and the Father who sent me has testified about me. But you have never heard his voice or seen his form, because you have not kept his message in your hearts. That is why you do not believe the one he has sent to you.

'You search the scriptures, because you think that in them you will find eternal life; and these very scriptures testify about me. Yet you will not come to me to receive that life.

'I do not need glory from men. But I know you; you do not have the love of God in you. I have come in my Father's name, and you do not accept me; but if someone else comes in his own name, you will accept him. How can you believe, if you accept glory from one another and do not look for the glory that comes from the one and only God?

'Don't think that I will accuse you before the Father. There is already someone to do that: Moses, in whom you have hoped. If you had believed Moses, you would have believed me, because it was about me that he wrote. But if you do not believe the writings of Moses, how will you believe my words?'

(JOHN 5:31–47)

JESUS REFUTES THE PHARISEES

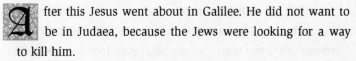After this Jesus went about in Galilee. He did not want to be in Judaea, because the Jews were looking for a way to kill him.

Then some Pharisees and scribes from Jerusalem came to him, and saw some of his disciples eat bread with unclean hands, that is, without washing them. Pharisees and Jews in general keep to the tradition of their elders, and do not eat until they have thoroughly washed their hands, or sprinkled themselves if they have come from the marketplace. And there are many other traditions which they have inherited and observe, about the washing of cups and utensils and bronze vessels.

So the Pharisees and the scribes asked Jesus: 'Why do your disciples go against the tradition of the elders, eating bread with unclean hands? They should wash their hands whenever they eat bread.'

Jesus replied: 'You hypocrites! Isaiah prophesied well about you when he said: "These people honour me with their lips, but their hearts are far from me. In vain do they worship me; the doctrines they teach are human ordinances."

'In fact, you break the commandment of God to cling to your merely human tradition, because he said through Moses:

"Honour your father and your mother; and whoever speaks evil of father or mother, let him die." But you say that if a man says to his father or mother: "Whatever you might expect from me is *korban*," that is, a sacrificial gift, he may not do anything more for them to honour them. You annul the word of God on account of the tradition you have received; and you do many similar things.'

Calling the crowd to him again, he said: 'Listen to me, all of you, and understand: nothing that comes into a man from the outside can defile him. It is not what goes into his mouth that defiles him; it is what comes out of him.'

Then the disciples came to him and said: 'Don't you know that the Pharisees were offended by what you said to them?' Jesus answered: 'Every growing thing which my heavenly Father did not plant will be uprooted. Leave them; they are blind leaders of the blind, and when one blind man leads another, both fall into a ditch.'

When he left the crowd and went into a house, the disciples questioned him; Peter asked him to explain what he had said. Jesus answered: 'Are you that slow? Don't you understand that nothing that goes into a man's mouth from outside can defile him, because it doesn't go into his heart but into his stomach, and from there into the sewer?' (This means no foods are unclean.)

'But the things that come out of a man's mouth come from his heart, and these are the things that defile him. From within, out of men's hearts, come evil intentions of fornication, theft, murder, adultery, greed, wickedness, deceit, calumny, lewdness, envy, blasphemy, arrogance and folly. These evil

92

deeds that come from within a man are what defile him; not eating with unwashed hands.'

(MATTHEW 15:1–20; MARK 7:1–23; JOHN 7:1)

THE WOMAN CONTENT TO EAT CRUMBS

Jesus left that place for the district of Tyre and Sidon. Wanting to see no one he went into a house, but could not be hidden. A Canaanite woman of the district whose daughter was possessed by an unclean spirit heard about him straight away, and began crying out to him: 'Pity me, Lord! Son of David, help me! My daughter is cruelly possessed by a demon.' But he answered her not a word.

His disciples came and urged him: 'Send her away; she keeps shouting at us.' Jesus answered: 'I was sent only to the lost sheep of the house of Israel.'

But the woman came in and fell at his feet and worshipped him, begging him to expel the demon from her daughter. She was a Greek, by race a Syrophenician.

Jesus said: 'Let the children be satisfied first; it is not right to take their bread and throw it to the dogs.' But she answered: 'Yes, Lord, but even the dogs eat the children's crumbs that fall from their master's table.'

Then Jesus said to her: 'Woman, you have great faith. Because you said this, let your wish be granted. Go now; the demon has left your daughter.' And she was healed from that hour; when the woman reached her house she found the child lying on the couch and the demon gone.

Moving again from the region of Tyre Jesus came through Sidon to the sea of Galilee in the middle of the Decapolis district. He went up the mountain and sat there, and great crowds came to him bringing people who were lame, crippled, blind and dumb, and many others. They laid them at his feet and he healed them.

Some people brought him a deaf man who spoke with difficulty, and begged Jesus to lay his hand on him. Jesus led him away from the crowd, on his own. He put his fingers into the man's ears and touched his tongue with spit; then he looked up to heaven, groaned, and said to the man, *Ephphatha*, which means 'be opened'.

At once his ears were opened, and the ligature of his tongue was loosed so that he spoke normally. Jesus ordered the man and those who were with him to tell no one. But the more he forbade them, the more eagerly they talked about it.

The crowd were astonished, marvelling at dumb people speaking, cripples made whole, lame people walking again and blind people seeing. They glorified the God of Israel, and said of Jesus: 'He has done all things well: he makes the deaf hear, and the dumb speak.'

(MATTHEW 15:21–31; MARK 7:24–37)

THE SECOND MIRACLE OF LOAVES AND FISH

gain there was a great crowd, and they had nothing to eat. Calling his disciples, Jesus said: 'I feel sorry for the crowd: they have been with me for three days now and have no more food. Some have come a great distance; I don't want to send them home without food, or they will faint on the way.'

The disciples answered: 'Where in this deserted place could anyone get enough bread to satisfy such a crowd?' But Jesus asked them: 'How many loaves have you?' They said: 'Seven, and a few fish.'

Jesus told the crowd to recline on the ground. Then he took the seven loaves and the fish, gave thanks and blessed them. He broke the bread and gave it to his disciples to distribute to the crowd, and the fish as well.

They all ate and were satisfied. Then they collected the pieces left over, seven baskets full. Those who ate were about four thousand men, and women and children as well.

As soon as Jesus had sent the crowd away he got into the boat with his disciples and came to the region of Dalmanutha, on the border of Magadan.

(MATTHEW 15:32–9; MARK 8:1–10)

NO SIGN FROM HEAVEN FOR FALSE TEACHERS

The Pharisees and Sadducees came to Jesus and began to debate with him. To test him, they asked him to show them a sign from heaven. Groaning inwardly, he answered them:

'Why does this generation want a sign? An evil and adulterous generation looks for a sign. I tell you truly, no sign will be given to this generation, except the sign of Jonah.

'When evening comes, you say: "Fair weather, because the sky is red." And in the morning: "Stormy weather today;

the sky is overcast and red." You know how to read the face of the sky; can't you read the signs of the times?'

Leaving them, Jesus and the disciples got into the boat again and made for the other side of the lake. When they reached it, the disciples realized they had forgotten to take bread and had only one loaf in the boat.

Then Jesus gave them a warning: 'Watch out for the yeast of the Pharisees and Sadducees, and of Herod.'

The disciples discussed what this meant, and decided he had said it because they hadn't brought bread. Knowing this, Jesus said: 'Men of little faith! How can you think it was because you're short of bread? Do you still not understand or grasp the truth? Have your hearts become hardened? Don't your eyes see or your ears hear?

'Don't you remember how many baskets of scraps you collected when I distributed five loaves among five thousand people?' They answered: 'Twelve.' 'And when I gave the seven loaves to four thousand: how many baskets?' 'Seven.'

And he said to them: 'Do you still not understand? How could you think I was talking about bread? But beware of the yeast of the Pharisees and Sadducees.'

Finally they grasped that he was warning them against the teaching of the Pharisees and Sadducees, not about yeast in bread.

(MATTHEW 16:1–12; MARK 8:11–21)

'I SEE PEOPLE LIKE TREES, WALKING'

When they came to Bethsaida, some people brought a blind man to Jesus and begged him to touch him.

Taking the blind man's hand, Jesus led him out of the village. He put spit in his eyes, laid his hands on them, and then asked him: 'Do you see anything?'

Looking up, the man said: 'I see people walking, but they look like trees.'

Again Jesus put his hands over the man's eyes. After that, the man looked straight ahead; his sight was restored, and he saw everything clearly.

Jesus sent him home, but warned him: 'Do not go into the village.'

(MARK 8:22–6)

PETER, THE ROCK ON WHOM JESUS WILL BUILD HIS CHURCH

Jesus went out to visit the villages of Caesarea Philippi. On the way he was praying alone, though the disciples were with him. Then he asked them this question: 'Who do the crowds say the Son of Man is?'

They said: 'Some say that John the Baptist has risen again; others, Elijah or Jeremiah or one of the ancient prophets.'

'But you,' he asked, 'who do you say I am?' Simon Peter answered: 'You are the Christ, the Son of the living God.'

Jesus responded: 'Blessed are you, Simon son of Jonah, because flesh and blood did not reveal this to you, but my Father in heaven. And now I say to you: you are Peter, and on this rock I will build my church; and the gates of hades will not hold out against it. I will give you the keys of the kingdom of heaven, and whatever you bind on earth shall be bound in heaven; whatever you loose on earth shall be loosed in heaven.'

Then he warned the disciples to tell no one that he was the Christ.

(MATTHEW 16:13–20; MARK 8:27–30;
LUKE 9:18–21)

JESUS FORETELLS HIS DEATH AND RESURRECTION

From then on, Jesus the Christ began to explain to his disciples that the Son of Man had to go to Jerusalem and suffer many things from the elders and chief priests and scribes: to be rejected by them and killed, and on the third day to rise again. He said all this openly.

Peter, taking him aside, began to remonstrate with him: 'God help you, Lord, this will never happen to you!' But Jesus, turning and seeing his disciples, rebuked Peter: 'Get behind me, Satan. You are an obstacle to me, because you think about human things, not about the things of God.'

(MATTHEW 16:21–3; MARK 8:31–3; LUKE 9:22)

JESUS' FOLLOWERS MUST SHARE HIS SELF-SACRIFICE

hen calling the crowd to him, Jesus said to them and his disciples: 'If anyone wants to be a follower of mine, let him deny himself and take up his own cross daily and follow me. Whoever tries to save his own life will lose it, but if he loses it for my sake and for the sake of the gospel, he will find it. What could anyone give in exchange for his soul? What good would it do him to gain the whole world and forfeit his own self?

'The Son of Man will come with his angels in his and his Father's glory and reward each man according to his conduct. If anyone of this adulterous and sinful generation is ashamed of me and what I teach, the Son of Man will also be ashamed of him.'

And he said to them: 'I tell you truly, there are some of those standing here who certainly will not taste death until they see the Son of Man coming in power in his kingdom, the kingdom of God.'[7]

(Matthew 16:24–8; Mark 8:34–8; 9:1;
Luke 9:23–7)

THE TRANSFIGURATION, VISION OF THE GLORY TO COME

ix days later Jesus took Peter and James and his brother John and led them alone up a high mountain to pray.

As he prayed, he was transfigured before them. His appearance was changed; his face shone like the sun. Even his clothes became dazzlingly white, whiter than any bleacher on earth could make them.

Peter and the others had been heavy with sleep, but when they saw the glory of Jesus they were wide awake. Then two men appeared, conversing with him: Moses and Elijah in glory, who spoke about his coming departure in Jerusalem.

When these two left him, Peter said to Jesus: 'Rabbi, Lord, it is good for us to be here. If you wish, let us make three tents, one for you, one for Moses and one for Elijah.' The disciples were so frightened that Peter didn't know what he was saying.

While he was speaking, a bright cloud came and overshadowed them, and they were afraid again as they entered the cloud. A voice came out of it, saying: 'This is my beloved Son, the chosen one in whom I am well pleased; listen to him.' Hearing this, the disciples fell on their faces in fear.

After the voice had spoken, suddenly Jesus was alone with them; looking up, they saw no one else. He came and touched them and said: 'Get up; don't be afraid.'

As they came down the mountain, Jesus said to them: 'Tell no one about the vision you have seen until the Son of Man has risen from death.' They kept it to themselves at the time, but discussed among themselves what rising from death could mean.

And they asked Jesus: 'Why do the scribes say that Elijah must first come?' He answered: 'Elijah is indeed coming first, and will restore everything. But remember what has been written about the Son of Man: that he should be despised, and suffer many things. I tell you, Elijah has already come, and they did not recognize him; they did what they liked to him, as scripture foretold. In the same way, the Son of Man is about to suffer at their hands.' Then the disciples understood he was speaking of John the Baptist.

(MATTHEW 17:1–13; MARK 9:2–13; LUKE 9:28–36)

EXORCISM REQUIRES FAITH AND PRAYER

When they had come down from the mountain and joined the other disciples, they found a big crowd around them and scribes debating with them. They were excited to see Jesus and ran to meet him.

He asked: 'What are you discussing?' A man fell on his knees, crying out: 'Teacher, Lord, I have brought you my son, my only child. I beg you, look at him and take pity on him; he is mad and sick. A dumb spirit seizes him, and suddenly he shouts; then it throws him down and injures him, and he foams at the mouth and grinds his teeth. Often it has thrown him into fire or water to destroy him. It hardly leaves him, and he is wasting away. I brought him to your disciples and begged them to drive the spirit out; but they couldn't cure him.'

Jesus said: 'Unbelieving and perverse generation! How long shall I be with you? How long must I put up with you? Bring your son to me.'

As they brought him, the spirit saw Jesus and at once threw the boy down violently. He lay writhing on the ground, foaming at the mouth.

Jesus asked his father: 'How long has this been happening to him?' He said: 'From childhood. But if you can do anything, have pity on us and help us.'

Jesus answered: '*If* I can? Everything is possible to one who believes.' And the father of the child cried out: 'I do believe! Help my unbelief.'

Seeing the crowd gathering, Jesus rebuked the unclean spirit: 'Dumb and deaf spirit, I command you: come out of him and never go into him again.'

Shouting and throwing the boy into convulsions, the demon came out of him. At first he seemed to be dead, and many said he had died, but Jesus took his hand and lifted him up. The boy was cured from that hour, and Jesus gave him back to his father. Everyone was deeply aware of the power of God.

When Jesus went into a house, his disciples asked him privately: 'Why couldn't we expel the demon?' He answered: 'Because you have so little faith. Truly I tell you, if you had faith the size of a grain of mustard, you would say to this mountain: "Move from here to there," and it would move; nothing would be impossible to you. But this kind of demon is driven out only by prayer.'

(MATTHEW 17:14–20; MARK 9:14–29; LUKE 9:37–43A)

JESUS AGAIN FORETELLS HIS PASSION

While everyone was marvelling at the things Jesus did, he and his disciples left that place and passed through Galilee. Jesus did not want anyone to know they were there, because he was teaching his disciples.

While they were walking in Galilee, he said to them: 'Keep in mind what I say: the Son of Man is about to be betrayed into the hands of men. They will kill him, but he will be raised up; three days after he dies, he will rise again.'

They did not understand these words; their meaning was veiled, and they were afraid to ask what he meant. But they were deeply grieved.

(MATTHEW 17:22–3; MARK 9:30–32;
LUKE 9:43B–45)

HE PAYS HIS TEMPLE DUES

When they came to Capernaum, the collectors of the half-shekel came to Peter and said: 'Doesn't your teacher pay temple dues?' He said: 'Yes.'

Jesus went ahead of him into the house and said: 'Simon, what do you think: from whom do the kings of this world demand toll or poll tax: from their sons, or from strangers?' He answered: 'Strangers,' and Jesus said: 'Then the sons are exempt.

'But so as not to offend them, go to the sea and cast a hook, and take the first fish that bites. Open its mouth and you will find a shekel in it; take it and give it to them for me and for you.'

(MATTHEW 17:24–7)

SPIRITUAL TEACHING

Humility

They came to Capernaum, and when they were in the house he asked them: 'What were you discussing on the way?'

They were silent, because they had started arguing about who was the greatest among them. Finally they asked Jesus: 'Who is the greatest in the kingdom of heaven?'

Knowing what they had in mind, he sat down, called the twelve to him and said: 'If anyone wants to be the first, he must be the last of all and the servant of all.' Then he called a child to stand next to him, put his arms around the child and said: 'I tell you truly, unless you change and become like children, you will never enter the kingdom of heaven. Whoever humbles himself like this child is the greatest in the kingdom of heaven; the one who is least among you is the greatest.

'Whoever welcomes a child like this in my name welcomes me, and whoever welcomes me, welcomes not me but the one who sent me.'

(MATTHEW 18:1–5; MARK 9:33–7; LUKE 9:46–8)

Tolerance

John said: 'Master, we saw someone expelling demons in your name and stopped him, because he is not one of us who follow you.' But Jesus said: 'Don't stop him; no one who does a deed of power in my name is likely to speak evil of me. He who is not against us is for us.'

(MARK 9:38–40; LUKE 9:49–50)

Kindness to God's Servants

'Whoever welcomes a prophet as a prophet will receive a prophet's reward; and whoever welcomes some righteous man because he is righteous will receive a righteous person's reward. And I assure you that if anyone gives one of these little ones a cup of cold water to drink because he is a disciple of Christ, that person will on no account lose his reward.'

(MATTHEW 10:41–2; MARK 9:41)

The Doom of Those Who Lead Others to Sin

He said to his disciples: 'Woe to the world because of scandals! It is impossible that scandals should not arise, but woe to the man whose conduct is a stumbling-block for others! It would be better for him to have been thrown into the sea to drown with a heavy millstone round his neck, than that he should bring down one of these little ones who believe in me.'

(MATTHEW 18:6–7; MARK 9:42; LUKE 17:1–2)

God Does Not Want One Person Lost

'See that you do not despise one of these little ones, because I tell you, their angels in heaven always see the face of my Father in heaven.

'What do you think: if someone has a hundred sheep and one of them strays, will he not leave the ninety-nine on the hills and go to look for the stray? I tell you truly, if he finds it, he rejoices over it more than over the ninety-nine who didn't stray.

'In the same way, it is not the will of your Father in heaven that one of these little ones should perish.'

(MATTHEW 18:10–14)

Reject What Leads You to Sin

'If your hand is the reason you sin, cut it off and throw it away: it is better for you to enter into life maimed than to go with both hands into the unquenchable fire of gehenna.

'If your foot causes you to stumble, cut it off and throw it away; it is better for you to enter into life lame than to be thrown with two feet into the eternal fire.

'And if your eye causes you to sin, pluck it out and throw it away. It is better for you to enter the kingdom of God with one eye than to be thrown with two eyes into the gehenna of fire, where their worm never dies and the fire is never put out.

'Everyone will be salted with fire. Salt is good; but if salt loses its saltiness, what will you use to season it? Have salt in yourselves, and live at peace with one another.'

(MATTHEW 18:8–9; MARK 9:43–50)

Point Out Your Brother's Sin

'Watch yourselves. If your brother sins, go and reprove him between the two of you alone. If he listens to you and repents, forgive him, and you gain your brother.

'If he does not listen, take one or two others with you so that the truth of every accusation may be established by two or three witnesses.

'If he refuses to listen to them, tell the church; and if he refuses to listen even to the church, let him be to you as the gentiles or the tax collectors.

'Truly I tell you: whatever you bind on earth shall be bound in heaven, and whatever you loose on earth shall be loosed in heaven.'

Then Peter asked him: 'Lord, how often must I forgive my brother if he sins against me: seven times?'

Jesus said: 'I tell you, not seven times but seventy times seven. If he sins against you seven times a day and tells you seven times that he is sorry, you must forgive him.'

(MATTHEW 18:15–18,21–2; LUKE 17:3–4)

United Prayer

'Again I assure you that if two of you on earth agree about anything you pray for, my Father in heaven will grant it; because where two or three have come together in my name, I am there among them.'

(MATTHEW 18:19–20)

God Shows Mercy to the Merciful

'This is how it is in the kingdom of heaven. A king decided to settle accounts with his servants. When he began, someone was brought to him who owed him ten thousand talents. Since he hadn't the money to repay the debt, the king ordered that the servant be sold, together with his wife and children and everything he had, to reimburse him.

'Falling to his knees, the servant did him homage and said: "Be patient with me, and I will repay you everything." Filled with pity, his master released that servant from his debt.

'But going out, the servant met a fellow servant who owed him a hundred denarii. Grabbing him by the throat, he said: "Repay what you owe me." Falling to his knees, his fellow servant begged him: "Be patient with me, and I will repay you"; but he refused, and had the other thrown into prison until he should repay what he owed.

'His fellow servants were greatly upset by what had happened, and came and told their master everything. So he sent for the servant and said: "Wicked servant, I forgave you all your debt because you begged me; shouldn't you have taken pity on your fellow-servant just as I took pity on you?"

'And in anger, his master handed him over to the torturers until he should repay everything he owed him. And that is what my heavenly Father will do to you, unless each of you forgives his brother from his heart.'

(MATTHEW 18:23–35)

JESUS' PRIVATE PILGRIMAGE TO JERUSALEM

The Jewish feast of Tabernacles was near, so his brothers said to Jesus: 'Leave this place and go into Judaea so that your disciples there can see the deeds you do. No one who wants to be known does such things in secret; if you really do them, show yourself to the world!' In reality, his brothers did not believe in him.

So Jesus answered them: 'You go up for the feast. I am not going yet because my time has not yet come, but you can go any time. The world cannot hate you, but it does hate me because I testify against it that its works are evil.'

Having said this he stayed in Galilee until his brothers had gone; then he did go, but secretly, not openly. So the Jews looked for him at the feast, asking: 'Where is he?'

Many in the crowds argued about him. Some said: "He is a good man"; others, "No, he is deceiving the crowds." But for fear of the Jews no one spoke openly about him.

(JOHN 7:2–13)

HIS TIME DRAWS NEAR: JESUS LEAVES GALILEE

When the time drew near for him to be taken up into heaven, Jesus committed himself to go openly to Jerusalem and sent messengers ahead of him.

They went into a Samaritan village to make preparations for him, but the Samaritans would not have him because he was on his way to Jerusalem.

At this the disciples James and John said: 'Lord, do you want us to tell fire to come down from heaven and destroy them?' But he rebuked them and they went to another village.

(LUKE 9:51–6)

BEING A CHRISTIAN REQUIRES SACRIFICE

While they were on their way a scribe came to Jesus and said: 'Teacher, I will follow you wherever you go.' Jesus replied: 'Foxes have holes and birds have nests, but the Son of Man has nowhere to lay his head.'

He said to another of the disciples: 'Follow me,' but he answered: 'Lord, let me first go and bury my father.' Jesus said: 'Leave the dead to bury their dead; you go and announce the kingdom of God.'

Another said: 'Lord, I will follow you, but let me first say goodbye to those in my house.' Jesus answered: 'No one who puts his hand on a plough and looks back is fit for the kingdom of God.'

(MATTHEW 8:19–22; LUKE 9:57–62)

THE SEVENTY-TWO FORERUNNERS

Then the Lord appointed seventy-two others and sent them ahead of him in pairs to every town and place he was going to visit.

He said to them: 'The harvest is abundant but the workmen too few, so beg the Lord of the harvest to send workers into his fields.

'Go now, but listen: I am sending you like lambs among wolves. Do not carry a purse or a wallet or spare sandals, and greet no one on the way.

'Whatever house you go into, first say: "Peace to this house." If a son of peace lives there, your peace will rest on him; if not, it will come back to you. And stay in the same house, eating and drinking whatever they eat; the workman deserves his pay.

'If you go into a town and they welcome you, eat what they put before you. Heal the sick people there, and tell them: "The kingdom of God has come close to you."

'But if you go into a town and they will not have you, go into the streets and say: "We shake off and leave with you even the dust of your city that sticks to our feet; but be sure of this, the kingdom of God is coming close."

'I tell you, that day will be more bearable for Sodom than for that town.

'Whoever welcomes and listens to you welcomes me, and whoever welcomes me welcomes the one who sent me. Whoever rejects you rejects me, and whoever rejects me rejects the one who sent me.'

(Matthew 10:40; Luke 10:1–12,16)

WOE TO THOSE WHO SEE MIRACLES BUT WILL NOT REPENT

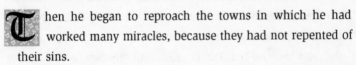 hen he began to reproach the towns in which he had worked many miracles, because they had not repented of their sins.

'Woe to you, Chorazin; woe to you, Bethsaida! If the miracles done in you had been done in Tyre and Sidon, they would have repented long ago, wearing sackcloth and sitting in ashes. Yet I tell you the day of judgement will be more bearable for Tyre and Sidon than for you.

'And you, Capernaum, were you to be exalted to heaven? You will be brought down to hades. If the miracles worked in you had been done in Sodom, it would still be standing today; but I tell you, the day of judgement will be more bearable for the region of Sodom than for you.'

(MATTHEW 11:20–24; LUKE 10:13–15)

THE REWARD OF THE SEVENTY-TWO

T he seventy-two returned with joy saying: 'Lord, even the demons submit to us in your name.'

He replied: 'I saw Satan fall like lightning from heaven. See, I have given you authority to tread on serpents and scorpions and on all the power of the enemy; nothing will ever hurt you. But do not rejoice because the spirits submit to you; rejoice rather that your names have been enrolled in heaven.'

Then Jesus, filled with joy in the Holy Spirit, said: 'Father, Lord of heaven and earth, I give you thanks and praise because you have hidden these things from the wise and intelligent and revealed them to infants. Yes, Father, this was your good pleasure.

'Everything has been delivered to me by my Father. No one but the Father fully knows who the Son is, nor does anyone fully know who the Father is, except the Son and those to whom the Son chooses to reveal him.'

Then turning privately to the disciples he said: 'Your eyes are blessed by what they see, and your ears by what they hear. I tell you truly, many prophets, kings and righteous people longed to see the things you see, and never saw them; to hear the things you hear, and never heard them.'

(MATTHEW 11:25–7; 13:16–17; LUKE 10:17–24)

THE CHRISTIAN'S PEACE OF SOUL

ome to me, all who labour and are burdened, and I will give you rest. Take my yoke upon you and learn from me, and you will find rest for your souls; because my yoke is easy, and my burden light.'

(MATTHEW 11:28–30)

WHO IS OUR NEIGHBOUR?

 lawyer got up to test Jesus by asking him: 'Teacher, what must I do to inherit eternal life?'

Jesus said: 'What is written in the law? What do you find there?'

He answered: 'You shall love the Lord your God with all your heart and soul, all your mind and strength, and you shall love your neighbour as yourself.'

Jesus said: 'You have answered rightly. Do this, and you will live.'

But he, wishing to justify himself in Jesus' eyes, said: 'And who is my neighbour?'

Jesus answered: 'A certain man was going down from Jerusalem to Jericho and fell among robbers, who stripped him of his clothes, beat him, and went away leaving him half dead.

'A priest happened to be going down that road, but when he saw the man he passed by on the opposite side. A Levite also came by and saw him, but passed on the other side.

'Then a Samaritan on a journey came upon him and was filled with pity. He went to him and bandaged his wounds, pouring on wine and oil. Then he put him on his own donkey and brought him to an inn, and looked after him. The next day he gave the innkeeper two denarii and said: "Look after him, and if you spend any more I will give it to you on my way back."

'Which of these three, do you think, became a neighbour of the man who fell among robbers?'

The lawyer said: 'The one who showed him mercy.' And Jesus said to him: 'Go and do the same.'

(LUKE 10:25–37)

WORK ISN'T EVERYTHING

On their way Jesus went into a certain village and a woman named Martha welcomed him into her house. She had a sister called Mary, who sat at the Lord's feet listening to what he said.

But Martha was distracted by all her chores, and said as she passed: 'Lord, doesn't it matter to you that my sister has left me alone to do all the work? Please tell her to help me.'

The Lord replied: 'Martha, Martha, you are anxious and disturbed about many things, but few are necessary – in fact, only one. Mary has chosen the better part, and it will not be taken from her.'

(LUKE 10:38–42)

THE FEAST OF TABERNACLES: DISSENSION ABOUT JESUS

I n the middle of the feast, Jesus went up to the temple and taught. The Jews marvelled and said: 'How does this man know what is written if he has never studied?'

Jesus answered: 'What I teach does not come from me but from the one who sent me. Those who try to do God's will can recognize whether my teaching comes from him or from myself. One who expresses his own thoughts seeks his own glory, but one who seeks the glory of him who sent him speaks the truth; there is no falsehood in him. Didn't Moses give you the law? Yet none of you keeps it. Why do you want to kill me?'

Someone in the crowd answered: 'You have a demon. Who wants to kill you?'

Jesus answered: 'Everyone is shocked because of one thing I did. But Moses – not really Moses, but the patriarchs – gave you circumcision, so you would circumcise a man even on the sabbath. If that doesn't break the law of Moses, why are you angry with me for healing a whole man on a sabbath? Judge rightly, not just by appearances.'

Some of the people of Jerusalem were saying: 'Isn't this the man they want to put to death? But he speaks openly, and they say nothing to him. Surely the authorities can't believe he is the Christ? After all, we know where this man comes from, but when the Christ comes no one will know where he comes from.'

So Jesus, while he was teaching in the temple, cried out: 'You know me, and you know where I come from; but I have not come of my own will. The one who sent me is true – the one you do not know. But I know him, because I have my being from him. It was he who sent me.'

They wanted to arrest him then, but no one laid a hand on him because his hour had not yet come. And many of the people believed in him; they said: 'When the Christ comes, will he do more miracles than this man has done?'

The Pharisees knew such things were being said, so finally they and the chief priests sent guards to arrest him.

That was when Jesus said: 'I will be with you only a little longer, and then I will go to the one who sent me. You will look for me, but you will not find me, and where I will be you cannot come.'

So the Jews asked one another: 'Where is this man going, that we won't find him? Surely not to teach Greeks in the diaspora? What does he mean by saying, "You will look for me but not find me," or "Where I will be you cannot come"?'

On the last and greatest day of the feast, Jesus stood and called out: 'Let anyone who is thirsty come to me and drink. As scripture says, rivers of living water will flow from the heart of whoever believes in me.' He was speaking about the Spirit whom those who believed in him were about to receive; they had not received him yet because Jesus was not yet glorified.

Hearing these words, some of the people said: 'This man really is the prophet, or even the Christ.' But others said: 'Surely the Christ couldn't come from Galilee? Doesn't scripture say he will be a descendant of David, and come from Bethlehem, where David lived?'

There was disagreement among them. Some wanted to arrest him, but no one laid hands on him.

The guards came back to the chief priests and Pharisees, who asked why they had not brought him. They answered: 'Never did anyone speak as this man speaks.' The Pharisees said: 'Don't tell us you have also been deceived? Has even one of the authorities or the Pharisees believed in him? This damned rabble knows nothing of the law.'

One of the Pharisees – Nicodemus, who had visited Jesus – said to them: 'Does our law judge any man without first hearing him, and knowing what he does?'

They answered: 'You're not from Galilee, are you? Search the records, and see for yourself: prophets do not come from Galilee.'

And then they all went home.

(JOHN 7:14–53)

THE WOMAN CAUGHT IN ADULTERY

Jesus, however, went to the Mount of Olives, and came back to the temple at dawn. All the people came to him and he sat and taught them.

The scribes and Pharisees brought him a woman who had been caught committing adultery. Making her stand in the middle of everyone, they said: 'Teacher, this woman has been caught in the act of adultery. In the law, Moses laid down that such people be stoned. But you, what do you say?'

They asked this to test him, looking for something to accuse him of. But Jesus bent down and wrote in the ground with his finger.

When they kept on questioning him, he stood up and said: 'Let one among you who is sinless throw the first stone at her.' Then he bent down and wrote on the ground again.

Hearing this, they went away one by one, starting with the eldest, and Jesus was left alone with the woman in the middle of the crowd. Standing up, he said to her: 'Woman, where are they? Has no one condemned you?' She said: 'No one, sir.' So Jesus said: 'Neither do I. Go now, and don't sin any more.'

(JOHN 8:1–11)

IT IS THE FATHER WHO BEARS WITNESS TO JESUS

Jesus spoke to them again, saying: 'I am the light of the world. No one who follows me will walk in the dark; he will have the light of life.'

The Pharisees said to him: 'You testify about yourself, so your testimony is not true.' Jesus answered: 'Even if I testify about myself, my testimony is true, because I know where I came from and where I am going; but you don't know where I come from or where I am going. You judge according to human criteria; I judge no one, but if I did, my judgement would be true, because I am not alone; the one who sent me is with me, and even in your law it is written that the witness of two men is true. I testify about myself, and the Father who sent me testifies about me.'

So they asked: 'Where is this father of yours?' Jesus answered: 'You know neither me nor my Father. If you knew me, you would also have known my Father.'

He said these things while he was teaching in the treasury of the temple, but still no one arrested him, because his hour had not yet come.

So he said to them again: 'I am going away, and you will look for me; but you will die in your sin. Where I am going, you cannot come.'

The Jews said: 'He's not going to kill himself, is he? Why does he say: "Where I am going, you cannot come"?'

But he said to them: 'You belong to the world below; I belong to the world above. You belong to this world; I do not. That is why I told you that you will die in your sins. If you do not believe that I AM,[8] that is what will happen to you.'

So they said: 'Who are you?'

Jesus answered: 'Why indeed do I speak to you at all? I have many things to say about you, and many things to condemn. But the one who sent me is true; and as for me, the things I say in the world are the things I heard from him.'

They did not know that he was talking about the Father.

So Jesus said: 'When you lift up the Son of Man, then you will know that I AM, and that I do nothing on my own; what I say is what the Father taught me. And he who sent me is with me; he has not left me alone, because I do only what pleases him.'

When he said these things, many believed in him.

(JOHN 8:12–30)

CHILDREN OF ABRAHAM, TRUE AND FALSE

T hen Jesus said to the Jews who believed in him: 'If you live by what I teach, you are truly my disciples. You will know the truth, and the truth will set you free.'

But they said: 'We are descendants of Abraham, and have never been slaves to anyone. What do you mean by saying we will be set free?'

Jesus answered: 'I tell you truly, whoever commits sin is a servant of sin. A servant does not remain in the family for ever; but a son does, so if the Son frees you, you will really be free.

'I know you are descendants of Abraham. But you want to kill me, because my teaching finds no home in you. I tell what I have seen with the Father, but you do what you have learned from your father.'

They said again: 'Our father is Abraham.' So Jesus said: 'If you are children of Abraham, do what Abraham did. But now you want to kill me, a man who has told you the truth he learned from God. This is not what Abraham did. You are doing what your father does.'

Then they said: 'We were not born of fornication. We have one father: God.'

Jesus replied: 'If God were your father, you would have loved me, since I come out of God and have come to you from him. I did not come of my own will; he sent me. Why don't you recognize what I tell you? Because you cannot take in what I say. You have been fathered by the devil, and want to do your father's will; he was a murderer from the beginning.

'He could never be believed, because there is no truth in him. When he lies he shows what he is: a liar and the father of lies. Because I speak the truth, you do not believe me. Which of you accuses me of sin? If I speak the truth, why don't you believe me? A man of God recognizes the words of God; the reason you don't is that you are not of God.'

The Jews retorted: 'Is it not well said that you are a Samaritan, and that you have a demon?' Jesus replied: 'I have no demon. I honour my Father, and you dishonour me. But I do not seek my glory; there is another who seeks it, and he is the judge.

'I tell you most truly, whoever does what I teach will never see death.'

Then the Jews said: 'Now we know that you have a demon. Abraham died, and the prophets have died, yet you say: "Whoever does what I teach will never see death." Surely you are not greater than our father Abraham, who did die? The prophets died too. Who do you claim to be?'

Jesus answered: 'If I glorified myself it would be an empty glory. My Father is the one who glorifies me, the one of whom you say: he is our God. But you have not known him, and I know him. If I said I did not know him, I should be a liar like you; but I do know him, and I do what he teaches.

'Abraham your father was glad that he should see my day; he saw it, and rejoiced.'

The Jews said: 'You are not yet fifty, and have you seen Abraham?' Jesus said to them: 'Very truly I tell you, before Abraham existed, I AM.'

Because he said this, they picked up stones to stone him. But Jesus hid himself and left the temple.

(JOHN 8:31–59)

THE CASE OF THE MAN BORN BLIND

While walking Jesus saw a man who had been blind from birth. His disciples asked him: 'Rabbi, who sinned, this man or his parents, to cause him to be born blind?'

Jesus answered: 'Neither this man nor his parents sinned. He was born blind so that the power of God could be revealed in him. While it is day, I have to do the deeds of the one who sent me; the night is coming when no one can work. While I am in the world, I am the light of the world.'

Having said this, he spat on the ground, made mud with the spit, put it on the man's eyes and told him: 'Go and wash in the pool of Siloam,' which means 'sent'. So the man went and washed, and came back with his sight restored.

His neighbours and those who had seen him begging said: 'Isn't this the man who sits and begs?' Some said: 'Yes, it is.' Others said: 'No, he just looks like him.' But the man himself said: 'I am the one.' Then they asked him: 'How were your eyes opened?'

He answered: 'The man called Jesus made mud, and put it on my eyes, and told me to go to Siloam and wash. So I did, and found I could see.'

They asked: 'Where is he?' He answered: 'I don't know.'

So they led the man who had been blind to the Pharisees. They again asked him how he could see, and the man said: 'He put mud on my eyes, and I washed, and now I can see.'

Now the day on which Jesus made the mud and opened his eyes was a sabbath, so some of the Pharisees said: 'This man is not from God, because he does not keep the sabbath.' But others asked how a sinner could work such miracles; so they were divided.

They asked the man who had been blind: 'What do you say about him, since he opened your eyes?' The man said: 'He is a prophet.'

But the Jews did not believe that the man who could see had been blind until they had sent for his parents and asked them: 'Is this your son whom you say was born blind? How is it that he can see now?' His parents said: 'We know that this is our son and that he was born blind. But how he can see now, we do not know; nor do we know who opened his eyes. Ask him; he is of age; he can speak for himself.'

The parents said 'he is of age; ask him' because they were afraid of the Jews, who had already agreed to expel from the synagogue anyone who acknowledged Jesus to be the Christ.

So the Pharisees again sent for the man who had been blind and said to him: 'Give glory to God. We know that this man is a sinner.' He answered: 'I don't know whether he's a sinner. All I know is that I used to be blind, and now I can see.'

So they asked him: 'What did he do to you? How did he open your eyes?' He answered: 'I've told you already, and you wouldn't listen. Why do you want to hear it again? Surely you don't want to become his disciples?'

Then they reviled him and said: 'You are that man's disciple; we are disciples of Moses. We know that God spoke through Moses, but we don't know where that man comes from.'

Then the man who had been healed said: 'What an amazing thing! He gave me my sight, and you don't know where he comes from. We know God doesn't listen to sinners, but if someone fears God and does his will, he hears that person's prayers. It has never been heard of that anyone restored the sight of a man born blind; if this man is not from God, how could he have done it?'

They answered: 'You were born a sinner through and through, and are you trying to teach us?' And they turned him out.

Jesus heard they had done this. He found the man and asked him: 'Do you believe in the Son of Man?' The man answered: 'Sir, tell me who he is, so that I can believe in him.' Jesus said: 'You have seen him; he is the one talking to you.'

The man said, 'Sir, I believe,' and worshipped Jesus. Then Jesus said: 'I came into this world to bring about justice: sight for those who can't see, and blindness for those who can.'

Some of the Pharisees who were with him heard this and said to him: 'Surely we are not blind?' Jesus answered: 'If you were blind, you would not be to blame for your sins; but since you say you can see, your guilt remains.'

(JOHN 9)

THE GOOD SHEPHERD

esus said: 'I tell you truly: anyone who does not enter a sheepfold through the gate but climbs in somewhere else is a thief and a robber.

'It is the shepherd of the sheep who goes in through the gate. The gatekeeper opens it for him, his sheep recognize his voice and he calls them by name and leads them out. Then he goes in front of them and they follow him, because they know his voice. They would never follow a stranger; they would run away from him. They don't recognize the voices of strangers.

'A thief comes only to steal and kill and destroy. I came so that they may have life, and have it in abundance.

'I am the good shepherd. A good shepherd lays down his life for his sheep. A hired man who is not the shepherd, to whom the sheep do not belong, leaves them and runs away if he sees a wolf coming, and the wolf seizes the sheep and scatters them. The sheep do not matter to him because he is only a hired man.

'I am the good shepherd; I know mine and mine know me, just as the Father knows me and I know the Father, and I lay down my life for my sheep. I also have other sheep that do not belong to this flock; I have to bring them in too. They will listen to my voice, and then there will be one flock and one shepherd.'

When Jesus told them this allegory, they did not understand what it meant. Then he said: 'I tell you truly, I am the gate of the sheepfold. Those who came before me were thieves and robbers, and the sheep did not listen to them. I am the gate; if anyone enters through me, he will be safe, and will go in and out and find pasture.

'This is why the Father loves me: because I lay down my life so that I can take it up again. No one takes it from me; I lay it down by my own choice. I have authority to lay it down and authority to take it up again, and this is what my Father commands me to do.'

Again the Jews were divided over these words. Many said: 'He has a demon, and raves. Why do you listen to him?' But others said: 'These are not the words of someone possessed by a demon. Could a demon open the eyes of blind people?'

(JOHN 10:1–5,10–18,6–9,19–21)

'HE EXPELS DEMONS BY THE POWER OF BEELZEBUB'

T hen they brought Jesus a man blind and dumb who was possessed by a demon. Jesus expelled the demon, and as it went out the man was healed and could see and speak again. All the crowd were astonished, and some of them asked: 'Could this be the Son of David?'

Hearing this, the Pharisees and the scribes who had come down from Jerusalem said: 'This man is possessed by Beelzebub, the prince of demons. He only expels demons by the power of Beelzebub.' Others, to test him, wanted him to show them a sign from heaven.

But he, knowing their thoughts, called them to him and spoke to them in parables. 'How can Satan expel Satan? If any kingdom is divided against itself, that kingdom cannot stand; it becomes desolate. Every city or house divided against itself falls; it will not be able to stand.

'You say that it is by the power of Beelzebub that I expel demons. But if Satan is expelling Satan, if he has risen against himself and is divided, how can his kingdom last? If I expel demons by the power of Beelzebub, by what power do your followers expel them? Let them judge you, then. But if I expel demons by the power of the Spirit – the finger of God – then his kingdom has overtaken you.

'When a strong, well-armed man guards his palace, his goods are safe; no one can enter the house and plunder his treasures unless he first ties the man up. But when someone stronger than him attacks and overcomes him, he takes away the weapons he relied on and then shares out his loot.

'Whoever is not with me is against me, and whoever does not gather with me scatters. I tell you truly, the sons of men will be forgiven all their sins and whatever blasphemies they utter, except blasphemy against the Holy Spirit. If anyone speaks against the Son of Man, it will be forgiven him; but if he blasphemes against the Holy Spirit, it will never be forgiven him, neither in this age nor the next; he is guilty of an eternal sin.' He said this because they had said: 'He is possessed by an unclean spirit.'

Then Jesus said: 'Keep a tree healthy and its fruit will be good; let a tree get sick and its fruit will be bad. A tree is known by its fruit. Offspring of vipers! How can you, being evil, speak good things? The mouth speaks out of the abundance of the heart: a good man says good things out of his store of goodness, an evil man evil things out of his store of evil.

'I assure you that on the day of judgement people will have to account for every idle word they have spoken. By your own words you will be justified, and by your own words condemned.'

(MATTHEW 12:22–37; MARK 3:22–30;
LUKE 11:14–23; 12:10)

DEMONS WILL RETURN TO AN EVIL GENERATION

When an evil spirit goes out of a man, he wanders through desert places looking for a place to rest, and finds none. Then he says: "I will move back into my house, the one I left"; and when he arrives he finds it vacant, swept clean and furnished.

'Then he goes to find seven other spirits more wicked than himself. He brings them with him, and they move in and live there; so the last state of that man becomes worse than the first. This is what will happen to this evil generation.'

(MATTHEW 12:43–5; LUKE 11:24–6)

MARY'S OBEDIENCE MORE BLESSED THAN HER MOTHERHOOD

While he was saying these things, a woman in the crowd called out to him: 'Blessed the womb that bore you, and the breasts you sucked!' But he said: 'Still more blessed are those who hear the word of God and obey it.'

(LUKE 11:27–8)

THE SIGN OF JONAH

hen some of the Pharisees and scribes responded by asking: 'Teacher, we wish to see a sign from you.'

With the crowds pressing on him, Jesus answered: 'This evil and adulterous generation seeks a sign, but no sign will be given to it except the sign of Jonah the prophet. As Jonah became a sign to the people of Nineveh by remaining in the belly of the sea monster for three days, so will the Son of Man be to this generation by remaining in the grave for three days.

'On the day of judgement, the queen of the south will be raised from death with the people of this generation and will condemn them, because she came from the ends of the earth to hear the wisdom of Solomon; but there is someone greater than Solomon here.

'On judgement day, the people of Nineveh will be raised to life with this generation and will condemn it, because they repented when they heard Jonah's preaching; but there is someone greater than Jonah here.'

(MATTHEW 12:38–42; LUKE 11:29–32)

THE WICKEDNESS OF THE PHARISEES AND LAWYERS

hile he was speaking, a Pharisee invited him to dinner; so he went to his house and reclined at table. The Pharisee was surprised to notice that Jesus did not wash before eating.

But the Lord said to him: 'You Pharisees clean the outside of cups and dishes, but within yourselves are full of robbery and wickedness. Fools! Didn't he who made the outside also make the inside?

'If you give to the needy from your hearts, everything will be clean to you. But woe to you Pharisees, because you give tithes of your mint and rue and every herb, but overlook justice and the love of God. You should give tithes, but not evade justice or charity.

'And woe to you for coveting the most important seats in the synagogues, and marks of respect in the marketplace. You are like hidden tombs that people walk over without knowing it.'

Then one of the lawyers spoke up: 'Teacher, when you say things like this, you insult us too.' But Jesus said: 'Woe to you as well, students of God's law, because you lay obligations on people that are a heavy burden to carry, and you don't lift a finger to help them.

'Woe to you for building tombs for the prophets, because it was your predecessors who killed them. That makes you witnesses who fully approve of what your ancestors did; they murdered them and you build their tombs.

'This is why God's wisdom says: "I will send them prophets and apostles, but some of them they will kill and persecute." This generation is guilty of all the blood of the prophets shed since the foundation of the world, from the blood of Abel to the blood of Zechariah who was murdered between the altar and the sanctuary. Yes, I tell you, their blood will be required from this generation.

'Woe to you, students of the law! You accepted the key of knowledge, but you yourselves did not go in, and you have stopped others from doing so.'

When he left that place the scribes and Pharisees became extremely angry, and tried to draw him out about many things so that they could trap him into saying something incriminating.

(LUKE 11:37–54)

DO NOT BE AFRAID OF HYPOCRITES

efore thousands of people so crowded together that they were treading on one another, Jesus first said to his disciples: 'Be on your guard against the leaven of the Pharisees' – that is, their hypocrisy.

'A disciple is no better than his teacher, nor is a servant above his master. At best the disciple is like his teacher and the servant like his master. If they call the master of the house Beelzebub, how much better are the members of his household?

'So don't be afraid of them, because nothing has been covered up that will not be revealed, and nothing hidden that will not be made known. The things we say in the dark will be heard in the light, and what we have whispered in private rooms will be proclaimed from the rooftops.

'Friends, let me tell you this: do not be afraid of those who kill your body and after that can do no worse, since they cannot kill your soul. The one you should really fear is the one who has power, after he kills you, to destroy both soul and body in hell. Yes, I tell you, fear him!

'Don't they sell two sparrows for a penny, and five for two pennies? Yet not one of them is forgotten by God or falls to the ground without his knowledge. So don't be afraid; you are worth more than many sparrows. Even the hairs on your head have been counted.

'I assure you that if anyone declares openly that he is a follower of the Son of Man, I will declare that he belongs to me before God my Father and his angels in heaven. But if anyone denies that he is a follower of mine, I will deny him before God my Father and his angels in heaven.

'And when they bring you in before synagogues and rulers and authorities, do not be anxious about how to answer them or what to say, because at that hour the Holy Spirit will teach you what to tell them.'

(MATTHEW 10:24-33; LUKE 12:1-9,11-12)

YOU CAN'T TAKE IT WITH YOU

Someone in the crowd said to Jesus: 'Teacher, tell my brother to divide our inheritance with me.' But he answered: 'Man, who appointed me a judge or arbitrator between you?' And he said to them: 'Watch out and guard against every kind of greed, because no one's life is measured by the abundance of things that belong to him.'

Then he told them a parable: 'A certain rich man's land produced big crops. So he thought to himself: I haven't enough room to store such a harvest; what shall I do? I know what I'll do: I will pull down my barns and build bigger ones to store all my wheat and my produce. Then I will say to my soul: You have enough laid up for many years to come; take it easy, eat, drink and be merry.

'But God said to him: Foolish man, this very night your soul will be demanded from you, and then these goods you are laying up: whose will they be?

'That is how it will be for one who amasses wealth for himself, but is not rich in God's eyes.'

(Luke 12:13–21)

JESUS WILL COME WHEN WE DON'T EXPECT HIM

ut on your belts and have your lamps burning like servants waiting for their master to come back from a wedding, so that when he comes and knocks they can open the door to him at once.

'Blessed are the servants the Lord finds looking out for him when he comes. I tell you truly, he will put on his belt and make them recline to eat, and he will come and serve them. Blessed are they if he comes at midnight or early in the morning and finds them still waiting.

'Be sure of this: if the master of the house had known at what time a thief was coming, he would have stayed awake and would not have let him make a hole through the wall. So be ready, because the Son of Man is coming when you least expect him.'

(Matthew 24:43–4; Luke 12:35–40)

WISE AND WICKED SERVANTS OF THE LORD

Peter said: 'Lord, is this parable for us or for everybody?'

Jesus answered: 'Who then is the wise and faithful steward whose master appoints him over his servants to give them their food at the proper times? Blessed that servant if his master comes home and finds him doing this. I tell you truly, he will put him in charge of all his possessions.

'But suppose a wicked steward says to himself: "My master is coming late," and he starts beating his fellow servants and maids, and eating and drinking with drunks and getting drunk himself. His master will come on a day and at a time he doesn't expect, and will cut him off and give him a place with unbelievers and hypocrites, where there will be wailing and gnashing of teeth.

'A servant who knows what his master wants but has not done it will be beaten with many strokes; a servant who doesn't know, but has done things that deserve a beating, will get fewer. Much will be demanded from anyone to whom much has been given, and still more if it was given him on trust.'

(MATTHEW 24:43–4; LUKE 12:35–48)

THE PRINCE OF PEACE BRINGS A SWORD OF DIVISION

'I came to set the world on fire, and wish it were burning already. I have a baptism to undergo, and how I am constrained till it is accomplished!

'Don't think I came to bring peace to the world; no, I tell you, but rather division. I came not to bring peace, but a sword.

'From now on a family of five will be divided three against two and two against three. I have come to make a son the enemy of his father and a father the enemy of his son, to turn mother against daughter and daughter against mother, a bride against her mother-in-law and mother-in-law against daughter-in-law. A man's enemies will be the members of his own household.'

And he said to the crowds: 'When you see a cloud rising in the west, you say at once that a storm is coming, and it does. When a south wind blows, you say it will be hot, and it is. Hypocrites! You know how to interpret the signs of the earth and the sky; why can't you interpret the signs of this time?'

(MATTHEW 10:34–6; LUKE 12:49–56)

REPENT OR PERISH

At this time some of those present told Jesus about the Galileans whose blood Pilate had mixed with their sacrifices. In answer, he said: 'Do you think those Galileans suffered as they did because they were the greatest sinners in Galilee? No, I tell you; but unless you repent, you will all perish as they did.

'Or those eighteen who were killed when the tower in Siloam fell on them: do you think they were more guilty than everyone else who lives in Jerusalem? No, I tell you; but unless you repent, you will all perish as they did.'

And he told this parable: 'A man had a fig tree in his vineyard, and came looking for figs on it, but found none. So he said to his vinedresser: Listen, for three years I have been looking for figs on this tree, and finding none. Cut it down; why should it take up space?

'But the vinedresser answered: "Sir, leave it for this year, so that I can dig around it and manure it, and see whether it will bear figs. If not, we can cut it down."'

(LUKE 13:1–9)

A CRIPPLED WOMAN HEALED ON THE SABBATH

esus was teaching in one of the synagogues on the sabbath, and a woman was there who had suffered from a spirit of weakness for eighteen years; she was bent double, quite unable to stand erect.

Seeing her, Jesus called her to him and said: 'Woman, you are freed from your handicap.' He laid his hands on her, and at once she straightened up and gave glory to God.

The ruler of the synagogue, angry that Jesus had healed her on the sabbath, responded by telling the congregation: 'There are six days on which we ought to work, so come to be healed on those days, not on the sabbath.'

But the Lord answered: 'Hypocrites! Which of you doesn't untie his ox or ass on the sabbath and lead it out of the pen to give it water? And this woman, a daughter of Abraham whom Satan has tied up for eighteen years: wasn't it right that she should be untied on the sabbath?'

When he said this, all those who opposed him were put to shame, and the whole congregation rejoiced over the glorious things Jesus was doing.

(Luke 13:10–17)

WILL ONLY A FEW BE SAVED?

esus travelled through towns and villages, teaching and making his way to Jerusalem. One of the crowd asked him: 'Lord, will only a few be saved?'

He answered: 'Fight to get in through the narrow door, because I tell you, many will try and won't succeed.

'Once the master of the house has got up and shut the door, those of you standing outside will start knocking on it, saying: "Lord, open for us." But he will answer: "I don't know you. Where do you come from?"

'Then you will begin to say: "We ate and drank with you," or: "You taught in our streets." But he will say: "I don't know where you come from. Get away from me, all who do immoral things!"

'Then there will be weeping and gnashing of teeth when you see Abraham and Isaac and Jacob and all the prophets in the kingdom of God, and yourselves turned outside. Others will come from east and west and north and south to recline at the feast in the kingdom of God; and you will see some who are now last who will be first, and some now first who will be last.'

(Luke 13:22–30)

PHARISEES WARN JESUS AGAINST HEROD

ust then some Pharisees came to him and said: 'Leave this place and go, because Herod wants to kill you.'

He said to them: 'Go and give that fox this message: See, I am expelling demons and curing the sick today and tomorrow, and will finish on the third day.

'But I must keep moving, today and tomorrow and the day after, because it is impossible for a prophet to perish outside Jerusalem.'

(LUKE 13:31–3)

'I AND THE FATHER ARE ONE'

hen came the feast of the Dedication in Jerusalem. It was winter, and Jesus was walking in Solomon's porch in the temple. The Jews surrounded him and said: 'How long are you going to keep our souls in suspense? If you are the Christ, tell us plainly.'

Jesus answered: 'I have told you, but you do not believe it. The miracles I do in my Father's name bear witness to me, but still you do not believe, because you are no sheep of mine.

'My sheep hear my voice; I know them, and they follow me. I give them eternal life; they do not perish for ever, and no one will snatch them out of my hand. My Father who gave them to me is greater than anyone, and no one can snatch them out of his hand. I and the Father are one.'

Again the Jews picked up stones to stone him. Jesus retorted: 'I have let you see many of the Father's good deeds; for which of them are you stoning me?' They answered: 'We are not stoning you because of any good deed, but for blasphemy; because you, a mere man, make yourself out to be God.'

Jesus answered: 'Is it not written in your law: I said, you are gods? If he called those who received God's word "gods", and scripture cannot be contradicted, do you tell the one the Father sanctified and sent into the world that he blasphemes because he said: "I am the Son of God?"

'If I do not do my Father's deeds, then don't believe me. But if I do, then even if you do not believe me, believe in these miracles. Then you will be convinced that the Father is in me and I am in the Father.'

When Jesus said this, they tried again to arrest him. But he escaped from them and left Galilee for the furthest part of Judaea beyond the Jordan, staying in the place where John had begun baptizing.

However, a large crowd followed him there and came to him. He taught them and healed them as his custom was, and people said: 'It is true that John worked no miracles, but every single thing he said about this man is true.' And many who were there believed in him.

(MATTHEW 19:1–2; MARK 10:1; JOHN 10:22–42)

ANOTHER SABBATH MIRACLE, BUT PHARISEES HAVE NO MORE TO SAY

esus went into the house of a leading Pharisee for a sab-bath meal. They watched him carefully, because in front of him was a man afflicted with oedema. So he asked the lawyers and the Pharisees: 'Is it lawful to heal on the sabbath, or not?' But they were silent.

Taking the man aside, he cured him, and sent him on his way.

Then he said: 'Which of you, if his son or even his ox fell into a pit on the sabbath, would not pull him out at once?' But they had no answer.

Then Jesus noticed how some of the guests were competing for the best seats. So he told them a parable: 'When someone invites you to a wedding reception, don't take the most impor-tant place at table. Your host may have invited someone more important than you, and he may come to you to say: "Give up your place to this person"; and then you will feel shame as you move to the lowest place.

'Instead, when you arrive, go and take the lowest place, so that your host may come and say to you: "Friend, come up higher"; then you will gain glory in the eyes of those at table with you. Whoever exalts himself will be humbled, but the one who humbles himself will be exalted.'

(LUKE 14:1–11)

NOT ALL ACCEPT INVITATIONS TO THE ETERNAL FEAST

Jesus also said to the man who had invited him: 'When you give a lunch or a dinner, don't invite your friends or family or relatives or rich neighbours; because if they invite you back, that will be your reward. When you entertain, invite poor people, crippled, lame and blind. Then you will be blessed, because they cannot repay you; so you will be rewarded at the resurrection of the just.'

Hearing this, one of those reclining with him said: 'Blessed is the one who eats bread in the kingdom of God.' So Jesus said to him:

'Someone gave a big dinner and invited many guests. When it was time to eat, he sent his servant to tell them: "Come now; dinner is ready." But as one man, they all begged off. The first said: "I have bought a farm and I have to go and look at it; please make my apologies." Another said: "I have bought five yoke of oxen, and I must go and try them out; please make my apologies." And another said: "I have just got married, so I can't come."

'When the servant came back and reported all this, his master was angry and told him: "Go out quickly into the streets and lanes of the town, and bring in the poor and the crippled, the blind and the lame."

'The servant came back and said: "Lord, what you ordered has been done, but there are still places." So his master said: "Go out to the country roads and lanes and compel people to come, so that my house may be filled. But I tell you all, not one of those who were invited will taste my dinner."'

(LUKE 14:12–24)

141

JESUS MUST BE MORE TO US THAN ANYONE OR ANYTHING

When a large crowd was following him Jesus turned to them and said: 'If anyone who comes to me loves father or mother more than me, he is not worthy of me. If he loves son or daughter more than me, he is not worthy of me. If he does not take up his cross and follow me, if he will not renounce[9] wife and children, brothers and sisters and even his own life, he is not worthy of me and cannot be my disciple. One who finds his life will lose it; one who loses his life for my sake will find it.

'If one of you wanted to build a tower, wouldn't he first sit down and work out the cost to be sure he had what was needed? If he laid the foundation and then could not complete the tower, everyone who saw it would laugh and say: This man began to build and couldn't finish.

'Or what king, preparing in time of war to fight another king, would not first sit down and carefully consider whether with ten thousand men he could stop the twenty thousand advancing on him? If not, he would send a delegation to sue for peace while the other was still far off.

'In the same way, any of you who will not let go of all his possessions cannot be my disciple. Whoever has ears to hear, let him hear.'

(MATTHEW 10:37–9; LUKE 14:25–33,35C)

GOD REJOICES IN PENITENTS, NOT THOSE WHO THINK THEY NEVER SIN

ow all the tax collectors and sinners were coming to listen to Jesus, and the Pharisees and scribes disapproved. They said: 'This man receives sinners and eats with them.'

So Jesus told them this parable: 'Which of you, if he has a hundred sheep and loses one, does not leave the ninety-nine in the desert and go after the one that is lost until he finds it? When he finds it, he carries it on his shoulders rejoicing; and when he comes into the house he calls together his friends and neighbours and says: "Rejoice with me, because I have found my lost sheep." So I tell you, there will be more joy in heaven over one sinner who repents than over ninety-nine righteous people who have no need of repentance.

'Or again, what woman with ten drachmae, if she loses one, doesn't light a lamp and sweep the house and search thoroughly until she finds it? When she finds it, she calls together her friends and neighbours and says: "Rejoice with me, because I found the drachma I lost." I tell you, this is like the joy among God's angels over one sinner who repents.'

And he said: 'A man had two sons. The younger said to him: "Father, give me the share of the property that would come to me." So he divided the estate between them.

'A few days later, when the younger son had got together all his possessions, he left for a distant country, and there squandered his property in extravagance.

'When he had spent it all there was a severe famine throughout that country, and he began to be in need. So he hired himself to one of the citizens of that country, who sent him into his fields to feed pigs. He longed to fill his stomach with the husks the pigs ate, but no one gave him anything.

'Coming to his senses, he said: "How many of my father's hired servants have plenty to eat, and here am I dying of famine! I will get up and go back to my father. I will say to him: 'Father, I have sinned against heaven and in your eyes; I no longer deserve to be called your son: take me as one of your hired servants.'" So he left to return to his father.

'While he was still at a distance, his father saw him and was moved with pity. He ran to him, fell on his neck and kissed him fervently.

'The son said to him: "Father, I have sinned against heaven and in your eyes; I no longer deserve to be called your son." But the father said: "Quick, bring out the best robe and put it on him; put a ring on his finger and sandals on his feet. Fetch the fattened calf and kill it. Let us eat and be merry, because this son of mine was dead and has come to life again; he was lost, and is found." And they began to celebrate.

'Meanwhile his elder son was out in the fields, but when he came near to the house he heard music and dancing. So calling to one of the servants, he asked what was going on, and the servant said: "Your brother has come, and your father has killed the fattened calf because he has got him back in good health."

'Then the elder son was angry, and did not want to go in. His father came out and pleaded with him, but he said to his father: "Look, all these years I have worked for you and done everything you told me to, but you never gave me so much as a goat to celebrate with my friends. And now that this son of yours has come after spending everything you gave him on prostitutes, you kill the fattened calf."

'His father said to him: "My son, you are always with me, and everything I have is yours. But it is right for us to be happy and rejoice, because your brother was dead and has come to life; he was lost, and is found."'

(LUKE 15)

INSURING OUR ETERNAL FUTURE

esus said to his disciples: 'There was once a rich man who hired a manager, and there were complaints against the manager for wasting his master's property. So the rich man sent for him and said: "What is this I hear about you? Show me the accounts; you can't be my manager any longer."

'The manager thought: "What can I do, now that my master is taking away my job? I can't dig, and I'd be ashamed to beg. I know what I will do, so that when I am removed from office others will receive me into their homes."

'Sending for each of his master's debtors, he said to the first: "How much do you owe my master?" He answered: "A hundred measures of oil." The manager told him: "Here, take your bond: sit down quickly and write fifty." Then to another: "And how much do you owe?" He said: "A hundred measures of wheat." He tells him: "Take your bond and write eighty."

'When the rich man heard about this, he praised the dishonest manager for his foresight. Indeed, the sons of this world

145

deal more shrewdly with their own kind than do the sons of light.

'So I tell you: use money, the mammon of the unrighteous, to make yourselves friends, so that when it no longer has any value they will welcome you into your eternal home.

'One who is honest in little matters is also honest in big ones; one who is dishonest in little things is dishonest in big things too. If you have not been honest about money, who will trust you with things of real value? And if you have not been honest about someone else's property, who will give you what is your own?

'No servant can serve two masters; either he will hate one and love the other, or be loyal to one and despise the other. You cannot serve God and mammon.'

The Pharisees, who loved money, listened to all this and scoffed at Jesus. So he said to them: 'You justify yourselves in the eyes of others, but God knows your hearts, and what people so admire in you is an abomination to him.

'The law and the prophets held sway until John; since then, the kingdom of God has been preached and everyone is pushing to get into it. But heaven and earth would pass away before one little stroke of the law lost its value.'

(Matthew 6:24; Luke 16:1–17)

THE RICH MAN AND LAZARUS THE BEGGAR

esus said: 'There was a rich man who used to wear purple and fine linen and feast splendidly every day.

'A poor man named Lazarus, covered with sores, had been laid at his gate. He hoped to satisfy his hunger with leftovers from the rich man's table, but only dogs came to him and licked his sores.

'Then the poor man died and was carried away by angels to the bosom of Abraham. The rich man also died and was buried.

'While he was being tortured in hades he raised his eyes and saw Abraham in the distance embracing Lazarus. So he called out: "Father Abraham, pity me; send Lazarus to dip the tip of his finger in water and cool my tongue, because I am suffering in these flames."

'But Abraham said: "Child, remember that you enjoyed good things in your lifetime while Lazarus had much to suffer; now he is being comforted here, and you are suffering. What is more, a great chasm has been set between us and you. If anyone wanted to go to you from here, he could not cross it, just as no one can cross from your side to ours."

'Then the man said: "In that case, Father, I ask you to send him to my five brothers in our father's house to tell them what he has seen, so that they do not also come to this place of torment."

'But Abraham answered: "They have Moses and the prophets; let them listen to them."

'The man replied: "No, Father Abraham, but if someone who has died goes to them, they will repent."

'He answered: "If they do not listen to Moses and the prophets, they will not be persuaded even if someone should rise from death."'

(LUKE 16:19–31)

FAITH AND GOOD WORKS

The apostles said to the Lord: 'Increase our faith.' He replied: 'If your faith were the size of a mustard seed, you would say to this mulberry bush: "Be uprooted and planted in the sea," and it would obey you.

'But which of you, if he had a worker ploughing or herding, would say to him when he came in from the farm: "Come up at once and recline at table?" Wouldn't you say to him: "Make me some dinner, then get dressed and serve me while I eat and drink; after that you can eat?"

'And would you thank the servant just for doing what he was told? It's the same with you. When you have done everything you were commanded to do, you should say to yourselves: "We are no profit to our master; we have only done our duty."'

(Luke 17:5–10)

TEN LEPERS CURED: ONLY A SAMARITAN THANKS JESUS

On his way to Jerusalem Jesus travelled along the border between Samaria and Galilee. As he came into a village, ten lepers stood at a distance and called out: 'Jesus, master, have pity on us.'

Seeing them, he called back: 'Go and show yourselves to the priests'; and as they went, they were healed.

One of them, when he found he was cured, came back

loudly glorifying God and prostrated himself at Jesus' feet and thanked him. He was a Samaritan.

Jesus said: 'Weren't all ten cured? Where are the other nine? Has only this foreigner come back to give glory to God?'

Then he said to him: 'Stand up and go on your way; your faith has healed you.'

(LUKE 17:11–19)

THE END OF THE WORLD

The Pharisees asked Jesus when the kingdom of God would come. He answered: 'The coming of the kingdom of God cannot be observed. No one will say: "Look, here it is, or there it is," because the kingdom of God is within you.'

Then he said to the disciples: 'A time will come when you will long to see the Son of Man even once and will not see him. People will say to you: "Look, here he is, or look there"; do not go after them. If they say: "Look, he is in the desert," don't go out; if they say: "Look, he is in these private rooms," don't believe it.

'When his day arrives, the coming of the Son of Man will be like lightning that flashes across the sky from east to west. But first he has to suffer many things and be rejected by this generation.

'As it was in Noah's time, so it will be at the coming of the Son of Man. Those who lived before the flood were eating and drinking, marrying and being given in marriage until the day when Noah went into the ark; they knew nothing until the flood came and killed them all. It will be the same on the day when the Son of Man is revealed.

'It will be as it was in the days of Lot; they were eating, drinking, buying, selling, planting and building. But on the day that Lot left Sodom, fire and brimstone rained down from the sky and destroyed everything. That is how it will be on the day when the Son of Man is revealed.

'On that day, if anyone is on the roof and his belongings are in the house, let him not come down to collect them. If someone is in a field, let him not turn back to fetch his things; remember Lot's wife! Whoever tries to save his life will lose it; whoever loses it will save it.

'I tell you, of two men in one bed that night, one will be taken and the other left. Of two women grinding together at the mill, one will be taken and the other left. Of two men in a field, one will be taken and one left.'

In response the disciples asked him: 'But where, Lord?' He said to them: 'Where the corpse lies, there the vultures will gather.'

(MATTHEW 24:26–7,37–41,28; LUKE 17:20–37)

GOD WILL DO JUSTICE TO THOSE WHO CRY TO HIM

esus told a parable to teach them to persevere in prayer without weakening. He said: 'In a certain town there was a judge who was not afraid of God or of what people thought of him.

'A widow of that town came to him saying: "Do justice for me against my opponent." At first he wouldn't do anything, but then he thought: "Although I am not afraid of God or of what people think of me, she is such a nuisance that I had better give her justice, or she will wear me out with her visits."'

The Lord said: 'Do you hear what the unrighteous judge says? Then will not God be patient towards his chosen ones who cry to him day and night, and give them justice? I tell you, he will do justice swiftly.

'But when the Son of Man comes, will he find any faith on earth?'

(LUKE 18:1–8)

THE SMUG PHARISEE AND THE CONTRITE TAX COLLECTOR

esus told this parable to some who had confidence in their own righteousness and looked down on other people.

'Two men went up to the temple to pray, one a Pharisee and the other a tax collector. The Pharisee stood and prayed privately in these words: "God, I thank you that I am not like the rest of men, rapacious, unjust, adulterers, nor even like this tax collector. I fast twice a week; I give a tithe of everything I get."

'But the tax collector, standing far back, would not even raise his eyes to heaven but beat his breast and said: "Be merciful to me, a sinner."

'I tell you, this man went home justified rather than the other, because everyone who exalts himself will be humbled; it is the one who humbles himself that will be exalted.'

(LUKE 18:9–14)

MARRIAGE AND CELIBACY

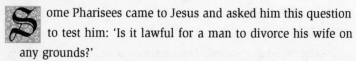

ome Pharisees came to Jesus and asked him this question to test him: 'Is it lawful for a man to divorce his wife on any grounds?'

He answered: 'What did Moses command you? Haven't you read that from the beginning, the Creator made us male and female?' And he said: 'Because of this, a man leaves his father and mother and is joined to his wife, and the two become one; they are no longer two, but one flesh. So what God has joined, let no man separate.'

They said: 'Moses allowed us to write a document of divorce and send our wives away.'

Jesus answered: 'He wrote this law because of the hardness of your hearts; in the beginning it was not like this. But I tell you that if a man divorces his wife – I don't mean a partner in fornication – and marries another woman, he commits adultery with her; and if a wife divorced from her husband marries another man, she too commits adultery.'[10]

Back in the house, the disciples questioned him about this. They said: 'If this is how it is between man and wife, it would be better not to marry.' Jesus answered: 'Not everyone will grasp what I said; only those to whom it has been granted.

There are celibates born that way from their mothers' wombs, and some who are made celibate by others; and there are those who choose celibacy for the sake of the kingdom of heaven.

'Whoever is able to grasp this, let him grasp it.'

(MATTHEW 19:3–12; MARK 10:2–12)

THE KINGDOM BELONGS TO THOSE OF CHILDLIKE FAITH

Then people brought children for Jesus to lay hands on them and pray for them. But when the disciples noticed, they rebuked them.

Jesus was angry when he heard this, and called the children to him, and said to the disciples: 'Let the children come to me; don't stop them, because the kingdom of God belongs to people like them. I tell you truly, whoever does not accept the kingdom of God as a child does will never be able to enter it.'

Embracing the children and laying his hands on them, he blessed them. Then he left that place.

(MATTHEW 19:13–15; MARK 10:13–16; LUKE 18:15–17)

INVEST IN HEAVEN: GIVE YOUR WEALTH TO THE NEEDY

As Jesus went on his way a young official came running, knelt to him and asked: 'Good teacher, what good deed should I do to inherit eternal life?'

Jesus answered: 'Why do you call me good or ask me about what is good? No one is good except God. But you know the commandments; if you want to inherit life, keep them.'

The man asked: 'Which?' Jesus answered: 'Do not kill, do not commit adultery, do not steal, do not bear false witness, do not defraud, honour your father and mother, and love your neighbour as yourself.'

But the young man said: 'Teacher, I have kept all these commandments from my youth. What do I still lack?'

Hearing this, Jesus looked at him and loved him, and said: 'There is still one thing you lack. If you want to be perfect, go and sell everything you have and give the proceeds to the needy, and you will have treasure in heaven. Then come and follow me.' But when the young man heard this he became sad, and went away unhappy because he was rich and had many possessions.

When he saw this Jesus turned to his disciples and said: 'I tell you truly, it is hard for the rich to enter the kingdom of God.'

The disciples were amazed, but he said again: 'Children, how hard it is to enter into the kingdom of God! I tell you, it is easier for a camel to go through the eye of a needle than for a rich man to enter the kingdom of God.'

At this the disciples were even more astonished, and asked themselves: 'In that case, who can be saved?'

Looking at them, Jesus said: 'To men it is impossible; but not to God. God can do everything, even what is impossible to men.'

(MATTHEW 19:16–26; MARK 10:17–27;
LUKE 18:18–27)

THE REWARD OF THOSE WHO LEAVE EVERYTHING TO FOLLOW CHRIST

R esponding to this, Peter said to Jesus: 'Look, we have left everything we own to follow you. What are we going to get for it?' Jesus answered: 'I tell you truly, in the resurrection when the Son of Man sits on his throne of glory, you who have followed me will sit on twelve thrones judging the twelve tribes of Israel.

'And if anyone leaves his house, wife, brothers, sisters, father, mother, children or fields for the sake of my name and the gospel and kingdom of God, he will get them back a hundred times over – houses, brothers, sisters, mothers, children and fields – even in this present time, though he will have to endure persecutions; and in the coming age he will inherit eternal life.

'But many who are now first will be last, and many now last will be first.'

(MATTHEW 19:27–30; MARK 10:28–31;
LUKE 18:28–30)

GOD DOESN'T HAVE TO TREAT EVERYONE EQUALLY

'The kingdom of heaven is like a man who went out early in the morning to hire men to work in his vineyard. He agreed with the workmen on a denarius for the day and sent them into his vineyard.

'Going out about nine o'clock he saw others standing idle in the marketplace, so he said to them: "You go into my vineyard too, and I will give you whatever is fair." And they went. Going out at midday and again about three o'clock, he did the same thing.

'About five o'clock he went out again and found others standing there. He said to them: "Why have you been standing here idle all day?" They said: "Because no one hired us." So he said to them: "You go into my vineyard too."

'When evening came, the owner of the vineyard said to his manager: "Call the workmen and pay them their wages, starting with those who came last and ending with those who came first."

'Those who came about five o'clock each received a denarius. Those who came first thought they would get more, but they also received a denarius each. They took it, but complained to the landowner, saying: "Those who came last worked only one hour, and you have paid them the same as us who bore the burden and heat of the whole day."

'Answering one of them, he said: "Friend, I am not doing you any injustice. Didn't you agree with me on one denarius? Take what is yours, and go. I chose to give this man who came last the same as I give you; haven't I the right to do as I please with my own money? Why should you be jealous because I am generous?"

'This is how those who are last will be first, and the first last.'

(MATTHEW 20:1–16)

JESUS BRINGS LAZARUS BACK TO LIFE

In the village of Bethany lived Mary, the one who anointed the Lord with perfumed oil and wiped his feet with her hair, and her sister Martha and brother Lazarus.

Lazarus fell ill, so the sisters sent a message to Jesus to say: 'Lord, the one you love is sick.' When he received it, he said: 'This sickness will not end in death; it is for the glory of God, so that by means of it the Son of God may be glorified.'

Jesus loved Martha and her sister, and Lazarus, but he stayed where he was for two more days and only then said to the disciples: 'Let us go back to Judaea.'

The disciples said: 'Rabbi, the Jews were wanting to stone you. Surely you're not going there again?' Jesus answered: 'Aren't there twelve hours in a day? When someone walks by day he doesn't stumble, because he has the light of this world to see by. It's when he walks at night that he stumbles because he has no light.'

Then he said: 'Our friend Lazarus has fallen asleep and I am going to waken him.' The disciples said: 'Lord, if he has fallen asleep, he will get better.' They thought he was talking about ordinary sleep, but Jesus was speaking of death. So he told them plainly: 'Lazarus has died. But for your sake I am glad I was not there, because now your faith will be strength-ened. Let's go to him.'

Hearing this, Thomas called the Twin said to his fellow dis-ciples: 'Let us go with him, so that we die with him.'

On the way Jesus heard that Lazarus had already been four days in the tomb. Bethany was less than two miles from Jerusalem, and many of the Jews had come to console Martha and Mary. When Martha heard that Jesus was coming, she went to meet him while Mary stayed in the house.

Martha said to him: 'Lord, if you had been here, my broth-er would not have died; but even now I know that God will grant you whatever you ask of him.' Jesus said to her: 'Your brother will rise again.'

Martha answered: 'I know he will rise again in the resur-rection on the last day.'

Jesus said: 'I am the resurrection, and the life. Whoever believes in me, even if he dies, will live; and those who live and believe in me will not die for ever. Do you believe this?' She said: 'Yes, Lord; I believe that you are the Messiah, the Son of God who was to come into the world.'

Then she went away and privately called her sister Mary, saying: 'The teacher is here, and he wants you.' When she heard that, Mary quickly got up and went to Jesus; he had not yet come into the village, but was still where Martha had met him. The Jews who were in the house to console Mary saw her get up and hurry out; they thought she was going to weep at the tomb, so they followed her.

She came to Jesus, fell at his feet and said: 'Lord, if you had been here, my brother would not have died.' When he saw that she was crying, as were the Jews who came with her, Jesus was moved and deeply saddened. He asked: 'Where have you put him?' They said: 'Lord, come and see.'

Jesus himself wept, and the Jews said: 'See how he loved him.' But some of them said: 'He opened the eyes of the blind man, couldn't he also have prevented this man's death?'

Still suffering inwardly, Jesus came to the tomb. It was a cave, and a stone was lying on it. He said: 'Lift the stone.' Martha said to him: 'Lord, it's the fourth day; by now he will stink.' But Jesus answered: 'Didn't I tell you that if you believe you will see the glory of God?' So they lifted the stone.

Then Jesus raised his eyes and said: 'Father, I thank you for hearing me. I know you always hear me, but I said this for the sake of the others, so that they will believe that you sent me.' Then he said in a loud voice: 'Lazarus, come out.' The man who had died came out, his hands and feet bound with bandages and with a cloth around his face. Jesus told the others: 'Unbind him and let him go.'

Many of the Jews who had come to Mary and saw what Jesus did believed in him; but some of them went away to tell the Pharisees what he had done.

(JOHN 11:1–46)

THE CHIEF PRIESTS AND PHARISEES DECIDE TO KILL JESUS

The chief priests and the Pharisees met together to consider their problem: 'What are we going to do, since this man performs many miracles? If we let him go on, everyone will believe in him, and the Romans will come and take away from us both our place and our nation.'

But one of them, Caiaphas, high priest that year, said to them: 'You know nothing; you don't understand that it is in our interest that one man should die for the people, rather than the whole nation perish.' He was not speaking in his personal capacity but as high priest, prophesying that Jesus was about to die for the nation; and not only for the nation, but to gather into one the scattered children of God.

So from that day they discussed ways of killing him, and Jesus no longer walked openly among the Jews. He left for a town called Ephraim in the country near the desert, and stayed there with the disciples.

The Jewish Passover was near, and people from all over the country were going up to Jerusalem to purify themselves before the feast. They looked for Jesus, and asked each other when they met in the temple: 'What do you think? Is there no chance he will come for the feast?'

(JOHN 11:47–56)

JESUS AGAIN FORETELLS HIS DEATH AND RESURRECTION

esus was on his way to Jerusalem, and those who followed him were astonished and afraid. Again he took the twelve aside and began to tell them privately what was about to happen to him.

He said: 'Listen, we are going up to Jerusalem and everything foretold through the prophets about the Son of Man is about to take place. He will be betrayed and handed over to the chief priests and the scribes. They will condemn him to death, and hand him over to the gentiles to mock and insult and spit at and scourge. Then they will crucify him; and on the third day he will rise again.'

But they understood nothing of this; his meaning was hidden from them, and they did not grasp what he was saying.

(MATTHEW 20:17–19; MARK 10:32–4;
LUKE 18:31–4)

TRUE AMBITION SEEKS ONLY TO SERVE

he mother of James and John, Zebedee's sons, brought them to Jesus and knelt before him. She said: 'Teacher, tell us you will do for us whatever we request.' So he asked: 'What do you want me to do for you?'

She answered: 'Grant that these two sons of mine may sit one on your right and one on your left in the glory of your kingdom.'

Jesus said to them: 'You don't know what you're asking. Can you drink the cup I am about to drink? Can you undergo the baptism I am about to undergo?' They said: 'We can.'

So Jesus said: 'You will indeed drink the cup I drink, and be baptized with my baptism. But places on my right or left are not mine to give; they belong to those to whom my Father has assigned them.'

When the other ten heard about this, they were angry with James and John. So Jesus called them to him and said: 'You know that those in power among the gentiles lord it over them, and their great ones make their authority felt. It must not be like that among you.

'Whoever wants to be great among you must be your servant, and whoever wants to be first among you must be everyone's slave – like the Son of Man; even he did not come to be served, but to serve, and to sacrifice his life as a ransom for many.'

(MATTHEW 20:20–28; MARK 10:35–45)

FAITH IN JESUS OPENS MORE EYES

esus and his disciples, accompanied by quite a crowd, were near to Jericho[11] when they passed Bartimaeus (son of Timaeus) and another blind man sitting at the roadside begging.

When he heard the crowd Bartimaeus asked what it was, and they told him Jesus the Nazarene was passing by. So the two men began to shout: 'Lord Jesus, Son of David, have pity on us.' Some in front of the crowd told them to be quiet, but they only shouted louder.

Jesus stopped and asked for the men to be brought to him, so they said to Bartimaeus: 'Courage, get up, he is calling you.'

Throwing off his cloak he jumped up and came to Jesus, who asked: 'What do you want me to do for you?' He answered: 'Rabbuni, Lord, that I may see again!' And they pleaded: 'Lord, that our eyes may be opened!'

Filled with tenderness, Jesus touched their eyes and said: 'See again. Go, your faith has healed you.' At once they regained their sight and followed Jesus along the road, giving glory to God; and all who saw it praised him.

(MATTHEW 20:29–34; MARK 10:46–52;
LUKE 18:35–43)

SALVATION COMES TO ZACCHAEUS

Jesus went into Jericho and passed through the city. A rich man named Zacchaeus, a chief tax collector, wanted to see who Jesus was, but he was short and the crowd blocked his view. So he ran ahead and climbed a sycamore tree to see him as he came past.

When Jesus reached the spot, he looked up and said: 'Zacchaeus, come down quickly, because today I must stay in your house.' He hurried down and welcomed Jesus with joy.

Seeing this, people complained: 'He has gone to stay with a sinner.' But Zacchaeus said in front of them all: 'Lord, listen, I will give half my possessions to the poor, and if I have extorted anything from anyone by false accusation, I will give it back four times over.'

Jesus said to him: 'Today salvation has come to this house, because even this man is a son of Abraham. The Son of Man came to seek out and save those who were lost.'

(Luke 19:1–10)

WE MUST MAKE GOD'S GIFTS PRODUCTIVE

After this he told them a parable, because he was near Jerusalem and they thought the kingdom of God was about to appear at any moment.

He said: 'A man of noble birth had to go to a distant country to be made king and then return. He called ten of his servants and gave each of them ten pieces of gold, and said to them: "Trade with these until I come back."

'But his future subjects hated him and sent a delegation after him to say: "We do not want this man to reign over us."

'When he returned after being made king, he sent for the servants to whom he had given the money, to find out what each had gained by trading.

'The first said: "Sir, your gold piece gained ten more"; so he said to him: "Well done, good servant. Since you have been faithful in a small matter, you will have charge of ten cities." Then came the second, saying: "Sir, your gold piece made five more." So he said to him: "You will be set over five cities."

'But the other servant came and said: "Sir, here is your piece of gold; I hid it in a piece of cloth, because I was afraid of you. You are a demanding man; you withdraw what you did not deposit, and reap what you did not sow."

'The king answered him: "Wicked servant, I condemn you out of your own mouth. So you knew I was a demanding man, withdrawing what I did not deposit and reaping what I did not sow? Then why did you not leave my money with a banker, so that it would have earned interest by the time I came back?"

'And to those standing by he said: "Take the gold piece from him, and give to the one who has ten." They said: "But sir, he has ten!"

'He continued: "As for my enemies, those who did not want me to reign over them, bring them here and kill them in front of me."

'So I tell you that to those who have, more will be given; but from one who does not have what he should, even what he has will be taken away.'

When he had told them this he went ahead of them toward Jerusalem.

(LUKE 19:11–28)

THE UNFORGETTABLE EXTRAVAGANCE

Six days before Passover Jesus came to Bethany, where Lazarus lived whom he had raised from death. While he was there they gave a dinner for him in the house of Simon the leper.

Martha served, and Lazarus was one of those reclining at table. Mary came to Jesus with an alabaster bottle of very expensive scent, pure nard. While he reclined she broke the neck of the bottle and poured the scent over his head and feet, filling the house with its perfume, and wiped his feet with her hair.

Some of the disciples were angered by this extravagance; they saw no reason for it, and were indignant with her. Judas Iscariot, the one who was about to betray Jesus, said: 'Why was this perfume not sold, and the money given to the poor? It would have fetched more than three hundred days' wages.' He said this not because he cared about the poor, but because he was a thief; he looked after the common purse and helped himself to what was put in it.

Knowing this, Jesus said: 'Why upset the woman? Let her be, she has done me a good deed. She was keeping this perfume to prepare my body for burial; all she did was to anticipate the day. You will always have the poor with you, and you can do good to them whenever you wish, but you will not always have me. She has done what she could, and I tell you truly, wherever in the world the gospel is preached, what she has done will be retold in her memory.'

Hearing that Jesus was there, a great crowd of Jews gathered to see him and to see Lazarus whom he had raised from death. The chief priests were considering killing Lazarus too, because on his account many Jews had left them and now believed in Jesus.

(MATTHEW 26:6–13; MARK 14:3–9; JOHN 12:1–11)

JESUS ENTERS JERUSALEM IN TRIUMPH

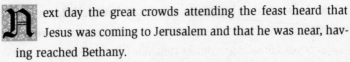ext day the great crowds attending the feast heard that Jesus was coming to Jerusalem and that he was near, having reached Bethany.

When he came to Bethphage on the Mount of Olives, he told two of his disciples: 'Go into the village opposite you. As you enter it, you will find a donkey tied up and with her a colt that no one has yet ridden; untie it and bring it to me. If anyone asks why you are taking it, say: "Because the Lord has need of it, and he will send it here at once."'

The disciples went and did as Jesus told them. They found the colt outside a door in the street. As they untied it, the owners said: 'What are you doing? Why are you untying the colt?' They answered as Jesus had told them: 'Because the Lord has need of it,' and they let them go. They brought the donkey and colt to Jesus and laid their cloaks on them. Then they set Jesus on the colt, fulfilling what had been foretold through the prophet: 'Tell the daughter of Zion, "Do not fear; look, your king comes to you humbly, mounted on a donkey; on a colt, the foal of a donkey."' While it was happening the disciples did not think of this prophecy; but after Jesus had been glorified they remembered that this had been written about him and about what they had done for him.

Those who had been with him when he raised Lazarus from death and summoned him out of the tomb had testified to the miracle, so as he rode a great crowd went out to meet him. Many spread their cloaks on the road; others cut palm fronds or branches from trees in the fields.

As he approached the descent of the Mount of Olives, the rejoicing crowd began to praise God loudly for the deeds of power they had seen. Those in front and those following him cried out: 'Hosanna to the Son of David, hosanna in the highest! Blessed be the coming kingdom of our father David! Blessed is he who comes in the name of the Lord, the King of Israel! Peace and glory in the highest heaven!'

But when Jesus came within sight of the city, he wept over it and said: 'If only you had known on this day the things that bring peace! But now they are hidden from your eyes. The days will come upon you when your enemies build a rampart against you, and besiege you and hem you in on every side. They will dash you and your children within you to the ground, and will not leave one of your stones on another; and all because you did not recognize the time of your visitation.'

As he entered Jerusalem, the whole city was in confusion, asking: 'Who is this?' The crowd answered: 'This is the prophet Jesus, the one from Nazareth in Galilee.'

He went into the temple and blind and lame people came to him and he healed them. But when the chief priests and the scribes saw the miracles he worked and heard children in the temple shouting, 'Hosanna to the Son of David,' they were incensed. They said to Jesus: 'Do you hear what these children are saying?'

He answered: 'Yes; and have you never read: "Out of the mouths of infants and babies still at the breast, you have brought forth praise?"'

Some of the Pharisees in the crowd said to him: 'Teacher,

rebuke your disciples.' But he answered: 'I tell you, if they kept quiet, the very stones would cry out.'

So the Pharisees said to one another: 'You see, there's nothing you can do; the whole world has gone after him.'

(MATTHEW 21:1–11,14–16; MARK 11:1–11A;
LUKE 19:29–44; JOHN 12:12–19)

JESUS ANNOUNCES HIS DEATH AND GLORY

A mong those who went up to Jerusalem to worship at the feast were some Greeks. They came to Philip, the disciple from Bethsaida in Galilee, and said: 'Sir, we wish to see Jesus.' Philip went to tell Andrew, and both of them went to tell Jesus.

Jesus said to them: 'The time has come for the Son of Man to be glorified. Very truly I tell you: unless a grain of wheat falls into the ground and dies, it remains alone; but if it dies, it bears much fruit. One who loves his life loses it, but one who hates his life in this world will keep it for eternal life.

'If anyone serves me, let him follow me, and where I am, my servant will be there too. If anyone serves me, the Father will honour him.

'Now my soul is troubled. What should I say: "Father, save me from this hour"? But it was for this that I came to this hour. Father, glorify your name!'

There came a voice out of heaven: 'I have glorified it before, and I will glorify it again.'

Hearing this, most of the crowd thought it must have been thunder, but some said: 'An angel has spoken to him.'

Jesus answered them: 'This voice came not for my sake, but for yours. Even now this world is being judged; now the ruler of this world is about to be expelled, and if I am lifted up from the earth, I will draw all people to myself.'

By saying this he signified the kind of death he was about to die. So some in the crowd questioned him: 'We have learned from the law that the Messiah remains for ever; how can you say that the Son of Man must be lifted up?'

Jesus said to them: 'The light will be among you only a little longer. Walk while you have the light, or darkness will overtake you; and one who walks in the dark does not know where he is going. While you have the light, believe in the light, so that you may become children of the light.'

When Jesus had said these things he left them; and when he had looked around at everything, it was late. With the twelve, he left the city for Bethany and lodged there, keeping himself hidden.

(MATTHEW 21:17; MARK 11:11B; JOHN 12:20–36)

BE PRODUCTIVE OR DIE: THE POWER OF FAITH

Early next day they left Bethany to go up to the city. Jesus was hungry, and saw a fig tree in leaf at the roadside some way ahead. When they reached the tree he went up to it as if to find something on it, but found only leaves; it was not the season for figs. He said to the tree: 'May no one ever eat from you; may you never bear fruit'; his disciples heard this. And the fig tree dried up instantly.

Early the following day, when they passed the fig tree again, they marvelled to see it withered to the roots, and wondered how this had happened. Peter remembered what Jesus had done, and said: 'Rabbi, look: the fig tree you cursed is withered.'

Jesus answered: 'Have faith in God. I tell you truly, if you have faith and do not doubt, you will do more than make fig trees wither. If anyone says to this mountain: "Be uprooted and thrown into the sea," and does not doubt in his heart but believes that it is going to happen, he will have his wish; it will happen. If you believe, you will receive whatever you ask for in prayer.'

(MATTHEW 21:18–22; MARK 11:12–14,20–24)

BY WHAT AUTHORITY DOES JESUS ACT?

They came again to Jerusalem, and Jesus went into the temple and walked as he taught the people and preached the good news.

The chief priests, scribes and elders of the people came upon him there and said to him: 'Tell us by what authority you do these things. Who is it that gave you this authority?'

Jesus answered: 'I will also ask you one question, and if you tell me the answer, I will tell you by what authority I do these things.

'John's baptism, where did it come from: was it from heaven, or from men? Answer me.'

They discussed his question, and reasoned: 'If we say from heaven, he will retort: "Then why did you not believe in him?"

But if we said from men, the people would stone us.' They feared the crowd, because the people were convinced that John was a true prophet.

So they answered Jesus: 'We do not know.' And he said: 'Then neither do I tell you by what authority I do these things.

'But tell me what you think of this: a man had two sons. He went to the first and said: "Son, go and work in the vineyard today." He answered: "I will, sir"; but he did not go. Then the man went to the other son and told him to do the same; he answered: "I will not go," but later he thought better of it and went. Which of the two did his father's will?'

They answered: 'The second.'

Then Jesus said to them: 'I tell you truly, tax collectors and prostitutes are going into God's kingdom before you, because John came to you in the way of righteousness, and you did not believe him; but the tax collectors and prostitutes did. And even when you had seen that, you did not change your minds and believe him.'

(MATTHEW 21:23–32; MARK 11:27–33;
LUKE 20:1–8)

MURDEROUS TENANTS OF GOD'S VINEYARD

Then Jesus began to speak to the people: 'Listen to another parable. There was a landowner who planted a vineyard, and planted a hedge around it and dug a winepress and built a tower. Then he leased it to tenants, and went away for a long time.

'When harvest time was near, he sent a servant to the tenants to receive from them his share of the produce of his vineyard. But the tenants seized and beat him, and sent him away empty-handed.

'So the landowner sent another servant; but they insulted and beat him too, and sent him away with nothing. He sent a third; they insulted him, wounded him in the head and threw him out. He sent another and they killed him; still others, and they flogged one, stoned another and killed the rest.

'The owner of the vineyard wondered: "What can I do?" He had one last person to send; his beloved son. He said to himself: "I will send my son; they should have some respect for him."

'But when the tenants saw the son, they said to one another: "This is the heir. Come on, let's kill him and take possession of the vineyard. His inheritance will belong to us."

'So they seized him, threw him out of the vineyard and killed him. When the owner of the vineyard comes, what will he do to those tenants?'

Some answered: 'He will put those wretched tenants to a wretched death, and lease his vineyard to others who will deliver its produce in season.'

Hearing this, others said: 'May it never happen!' Jesus looked at them and said: 'What does scripture say? Have you never read: "A stone which the builders rejected became the cornerstone; this was the Lord's deed, and it is marvellous in our eyes?"

'Whoever trips on that stone will be broken in pieces, and if it falls on anyone it will crush him to powder. So I tell you, the kingdom of God will be taken from you and given to a nation that will yield its produce.'

Hearing this, the chief priests and the Pharisees knew that he had told this parable about them; and the scribes and chief priests wanted to arrest him at once. But they were afraid of the crowd, because the people regarded Jesus as a prophet. So they left him and went away.

(MATTHEW 21:33–46; MARK 12:1–12;
LUKE 20:9–19)

GOD'S INVITATIONS SCORNED

In response, Jesus again spoke to them in parables, saying: 'The kingdom of heaven is like a king who gave a wedding reception for his son. But when he sent his servants to call those invited to the feast, they did not want to come.

'He sent other servants, saying: "Tell those who were invited: 'Look, I have prepared my dinner; my oxen and fatted calves have been killed, and everything is ready. Come to the feast.'"

'But they didn't care; one went away to his field, another to his business, and the rest seized the king's servants and insulted and killed them.

'So the king became angry; he sent his soldiers to execute those murderers and burn their city.

'Then he said to his servants: "The feast is ready, but those invited were not worthy, so go into the city squares and call to the feast everyone you find."

'The servants went into the streets and brought in everyone they found, both bad and good, so that the wedding hall was filled with people reclining at table.

'But when the king came in to see them, he noticed a man not wearing a wedding robe. So he said to him: "Friend, how did you get in without a wedding robe?" But the man had nothing to say.

'Then the king said to the servants: "Bind him hand and foot and throw him into the outer darkness, where there will be wailing and gnashing of teeth." Because many are called, but few are chosen.'

(MATTHEW 22:1–14)

DUTY TO THE STATE AND DUTY TO GOD

T hen the Pharisees met to consider how they might trap Jesus into saying something for which they could hand him over to the authority and power of the governor. Watching carefully for their opportunity, they sent spies to him who pretended to be righteous men: some of their own followers, and some of the Herodians.

They came to put a question to him, and said: 'Teacher, we know that you speak the truth and rightly teach the way of God, and that no one stops you speaking your mind, because you are no respecter of persons. So tell us what you think: is it lawful for us to pay tax to the emperor, or not? May we pay it, or must we refuse?'

Jesus, perceiving their slyness, said: 'Why do you hypocrites put me to the test? Show me the money with which the tax is paid; bring me a denarius.' So they did. He said: 'Whose image and title is this?' They said: 'Caesar's.' Jesus said: 'Then give to Caesar what belongs to him, and give to God what belongs to God.'

In front of everyone, they had failed to trap Jesus; he had silenced them. They themselves went away marvelling at his answer.

(MATTHEW 22:15–22; MARK 12:13–17;
LUKE 20:20–26)

THE SADDUCEES SILENCED: THE DEAD DO RISE AGAIN

The same day some Sadducees, who deny that there is a resurrection, came to Jesus and put this question to him: 'Teacher, Moses taught us that if a man dies childless, his brother should marry his widow and father children for him.

'Now suppose there were seven brothers. The first married and died childless, leaving his wife to his brother. He married her and died childless. The third married her, and so it went on until all seven brothers had died, leaving no children. Last of all the wife died. So when they rise again in the resurrection, whose wife will she be, since all seven had been married to her?'

Jesus answered them: 'How wrong you are; you know neither the scriptures nor the power of God. The children of this present age marry and are given in marriage; but those who are found worthy of the age of the resurrection, after they rise again from death, neither marry nor are given in marriage; they are immortal, like the angels in heaven, and as children of the resurrection they are children of God alone.

'And concerning the resurrection of the dead: haven't you read, in the passage about Moses at the bush, how he emphasizes what God said to him and to you: "I am the God of Abraham, and the God of Isaac, and the God of Jacob"? Moses calls the Lord the God of Abraham and Isaac and Jacob, but he is the God of living people, not dead; to him, everyone is alive. You are so wrong!'

Hearing his teaching, the crowds were astonished. Even some of the scribes said: 'Teacher, well spoken,' and from then on they did not dare to argue with him.

(MATTHEW 22:23–33; MARK 12:18–27;
LUKE 20:27–40)

THE GREATEST OF GOD'S COMMANDMENTS

ow the Pharisees gathered, having heard how Jesus had silenced the Sadducees. One of them, a scribe and lawyer, heard the debate and how well Jesus had answered them.

He came up to test him with a question: 'Teacher, which commandment is the first and greatest of all in the law?'

Jesus answered: 'The first is this: "Listen, Israel: the Lord our God is one Lord, and you shall love the Lord your God with your whole heart and soul, with all your understanding and strength." This is the first and greatest commandment.

'The second is like it: "You shall love your neighbour as yourself." There are no commandments greater than these two;

the whole law depends on them, and the prophets as well.'

The scribe answered: 'Well said, teacher; in truth there is one God, and no other beside him. To love him with all our heart and understanding and strength, and love our neighbour as we love ourselves, is worth more than all the burnt offerings and sacrifices.'

Seeing that he answered with understanding, Jesus said to him: 'You are not far from the kingdom of God.' And no one dared to question him any more.

(MATTHEW 22:34–40; MARK 12:28–34)

THE PHARISEES SILENCED AGAIN: DAVID CALLS THE MESSIAH 'LORD'

Jesus put a question to the Pharisees who were gathered in the temple where he was teaching: 'What do you think about the Messiah: from whom is he descended?' They answered: 'From David.'

Jesus replied: 'But how can the scribes say that? David himself, inspired by the Holy Spirit, says in the book of Psalms: "The Lord said to my Lord: sit on my right, while I make your enemies a footstool under your feet." If David calls the Messiah "Lord", in what way is he David's descendant?'

No one had a word to say, and from that day on they did not dare to dispute with him. But big crowds were happy to listen to him.

(MATTHEW 22:41–6; MARK 12:35–7;
LUKE 20:41–4)

JESUS CONDEMNS THE SCRIBES AND PHARISEES

While he was teaching, Jesus said to his disciples in the hearing of all the people: 'Beware of the scribes. They and the Pharisees sit on the seat of Moses, so you must listen to what they say and do as they tell you.

'But do not copy what they do, because that is not what they teach. They tie up heavy burdens to lay on the shoulders of others, but they won't lift a finger to help them; they devour the property of widows. They do it on the pretext of long prayers, and for this their judgement will be all the more severe.

'Everything they do is done to be seen. They like to walk about in long robes and enlarge their phylacteries and fringes. They want the most important places at dinners and in the synagogues. They like to be greeted in the marketplaces, and to be called rabbi.

'But you are not to be called rabbi, because you have only one teacher, and all of you are pupils. Call no one your father on earth, because you all have one Father in heaven. Nor must any of you be called leaders, because you have only one leader, the Christ.

'The greatest among you is to be your servant. Whoever exalts himself will be humbled; the one who humbles himself will be exalted.

'Woe to you, scribes and Pharisees, hypocrites! You shut the kingdom of heaven to others – you don't go in yourselves, and you won't let others go in who want to.

'Woe to you, scribes and Pharisees, hypocrites! You travel over land and sea to make one convert, but when he becomes a Jew you make him twice as much a child of hell as you are.

'Woe to you, blind leaders who say: "If you swear by the temple, your oath has no force; but if you swear by the gold of the temple, you are bound by it." Blind fools! Which is greater, the gold or the temple that makes it sacred? You say: "If you swear by the altar, your oath has no force; but swear by the offering on the altar, and you are bound." You are blind! Which is greater, the gift or the altar that makes it holy?

'If you swear by the altar, you swear by it and by everything on it; if you swear by the temple, you swear by it and by the one who lives in it. And if you swear by heaven, you swear by the throne of God and by the one who sits on it.

'Woe to you, scribes and Pharisees, hypocrites! You tithe your mint and dill and cummin, but neglect the major precepts of the law about justice, mercy and the fulfilment of contracts. You should have obeyed these, without neglecting the lesser precepts. Blind leaders! You strain out gnats, but swallow camels.

'Woe to you, scribes and Pharisees, hypocrites! You clean the outside of cup and dish while the inside is full of robbery and intemperance. Blind Pharisee! First clean the inside of the cup; then the outside can also be clean.

'Woe to you, scribes and Pharisees, hypocrites! You are like whitewashed tombs, beautiful on the outside but full of dead men's bones and uncleanness of every kind. You seem righteous to others, but inwardly you are full of hypocrisy and lawlessness.

'Woe to you, scribes and Pharisees, hypocrites! You build the tombs of the prophets and decorate monuments to righteous people, and say: "If we had lived in the days of our fathers, we would not have shared their guilt in the blood of the prophets." So you yourselves testify that you are your fathers' sons, and you complete what your fathers began.

'Snakes! Viper's brood! How will you escape being damned to hell? This is why I send you prophets and wise men and scribes, but some of them you will kill and crucify, and others you will scourge in your synagogues and hunt from town to town. In this way you will become guilty of all the righteous blood shed on the earth, from the blood of the righteous Abel to the blood of Zechariah the son of Barachiah whom you murdered between the sanctuary and the altar. I tell you truly, all this guilt will come upon this generation.

'Jerusalem, Jerusalem, you kill the prophets and stone those sent to you. How often I wanted to gather your children as a hen gathers her chickens under her wings; but you did not want it. So now your house is left to you, because I tell you, you will not see me again until the time when you say: "Blessed is he who comes in the name of the Lord."'

(MATTHEW 23; MARK 12:38–40;

LUKE 13:34–5; 20:45–7)

THE WOMAN WHO GAVE HER LAST TWO COINS TO GOD

Sitting opposite the temple treasury, Jesus watched people putting donations into the collecting box. Many rich people put in large amounts.

Then a poor widow came and he saw her put in two small coins. Calling his disciples to him, he said: 'I tell you truly, that poor widow put more into the treasury than all the others; because they contributed out of what they had to spare, but out of her poverty she put in everything she had, all she had to live on.'

(MARK 12:41–4; LUKE 21:1–4)

WHY MANY WOULD NOT BELIEVE IN JESUS

Many people did not believe in Jesus, though they had seen him work many miracles. They fulfilled the saying of Isaiah the prophet: 'Lord, who has believed our message, and to whom was the power of your arm revealed?'

They could not believe, because as Isaiah said: 'He has blinded their eyes and hardened their hearts; otherwise they might have seen with their eyes and understood with their hearts and been converted, and I would have healed them.' Isaiah said this because he saw his glory, and spoke about him.

Nevertheless, even among the authorities, many did believe in Jesus; but because of the Pharisees, they did not profess their belief for fear of being expelled from the synagogue. They valued public approval more than the approval of God.

But Jesus cried out and said: 'Whoever believes in me believes, not in me, but in the one who sent me. I have come into the world as a light, so that whoever believes in me does not remain in the dark.

'And if someone hears my words and does not act on them, I do not judge him. I did not come to judge the world, but to save it. Whoever rejects me and does not accept what I say has another judge; the very message I brought will be his judge on the last day. Because I have not spoken on my own initiative; the Father who sent me has told me what I may say and what I should speak about. And I know that eternal life means doing his will, so I say only what the Father has told me to say.'

(JOHN 12:37–50)

JESUS FORETELLS THE DESTRUCTION OF JERUSALEM

As Jesus left the temple, his disciples came to him and one said: 'Look, teacher: what great stones, what great buildings!' And they remarked on the beautiful stones and gifts with which the temple had been decorated.

Jesus answered: 'You admire these buildings and decorations? I tell you truly, a time is coming when they will be completely destroyed. Not one stone will be left standing on another.'

Later, he was sitting on the Mount of Olives opposite the temple and Peter, James, John and Andrew came to ask him privately: 'Tell us, teacher, when this will happen, and what sign there will be that it is about to happen. What will be the sign of your coming, and of the end of the age?'

In answer, Jesus said: 'Watch out that no one deceives you; do not be led astray, because many will come in my name saying: "I am the Christ," or: "The time is near." Do not go after them; they will mislead many.'

Then he said to them: 'You will hear news of riots and wars, but don't be afraid; these things must happen first, but the end will not come at once. Nation will rise against nation and kingdom against kingdom, and there will be great earthquakes and plagues and famines in different places, and signs from heaven; but these things are only the first pains of birth.

'Watch out for yourselves and be on your guard, because before these things happen men will persecute and seize you, and hand you over to synagogues and councils and prisons, and beat and scourge you in their synagogues. On my account you will be brought before governors and kings, but this will be your opportunity to testify to them and to the gentiles, because the gospel of the kingdom has to be proclaimed throughout the world as a testimony for all the nations. Only then will the end come.

'But keep this in mind: do not be anxious or rehearse your defence before you are brought to trial, because what you are to say will be put into your minds when the time comes. I will give you an eloquence and wisdom which none of your opponents will be able to resist or contradict, because it will not be you who are speaking, but the Holy Spirit of your Father within you.

'You will be betrayed even by parents and brothers, relatives and friends. Brother will betray brother to death, and fathers their children; children will turn against their parents and put them to death. They will hand you over to be tortured, and will kill some of you. You will be hated by people of every nation on my account. Many will give up the faith, and betray and hate one another; false prophets will arise and lead many astray. As lawlessness grows, the love of many will grow cold.

'But not a hair of your heads will be lost; by enduring to the end, you will save your souls. When they persecute you in one town, take refuge in another. I assure you that you will not have done the round of the towns of Israel before the Son of Man intervenes.[12]

'When you see the abomination of desolation that was foretold through the prophet Daniel standing in the sanctuary where it should never stand' – let the reader understand this – 'those in Judaea must escape into the hills. Those in the city must leave it, and those in the country must not go into it. A man on the roof of his house must not go down to take anything out of it, nor a man in the field fetch a cloak from the things he has left behind.

'Pray that you do not have to escape in winter, or on the sabbath. It will be hard in those days for women who are pregnant or nursing babies, because they are days of vengeance in which everything foretold in scripture will be fulfilled.

'There will be great distress in the land and wrath against this people, and they will fall by the edge of the sword or be led away as captives to all the nations. Jerusalem will be trodden down by gentiles until the age of the gentiles is over. But when these things begin to happen, stand erect and lift up your heads, because your redemption is near.'

And he said to them: 'Learn a parable from the fig tree, and all the trees. When you see their branches become tender and burst into leaf, you know that the summer is near. In the same way, when you see these things happening, you will know that the kingdom of God is near – at the very doors. I tell you truly, this generation will certainly not pass away until all these things have happened.

'Heaven and earth will pass away, but my words will never pass away.'

(MATTHEW 10:17–23; 24:1–20,32–5; MARK 13:1–18,28–31; LUKE 21:5–24,28–33)

THE END OF THIS WORLD AND THE COMING OF CHRIST IN GLORY

'There will be a time of great affliction, once and never again, of a kind never known since God created the world. If he were not to cut those days short, no one alive would be saved; but for the sake of his chosen ones, he will shorten them.

'If at that time anyone tells you: "See, here is the Christ," or "Look, there he is," do not believe him. False Christs and false prophets will appear and perform great signs and wonders to lead astray, if possible, even God's chosen ones. But you will recognize them, because I have warned you in advance.

'Immediately after the affliction of that time there will be signs in the sky: the sun will be darkened, the moon will not give her light and the stars will fall. The nations of the world will be anxious and perplexed at the sound of sea and its waves, and people will faint from fear and expectation of what will happen to the earth, because the powers of the universe will be shaken.

'Then the sign of the Son of Man will appear in heaven, and all the tribes of the earth will lament; and they will see the Son of Man coming on the clouds of heaven with great power and glory. With the blast of a great trumpet he will send his angels to gather his chosen ones from the four points of the compass, from the ends of the earth to the ends of heaven.

'So keep awake and watch, because you do not know the day or the hour when your Lord is coming. No one knows it, not the angels in heaven nor even the Son;[13] only the Father. So be watchful at all times, begging that you may be able to escape the coming dangers and stand before the Son of Man.

'And watch yourselves; do not let your hearts be burdened by debauchery and drunkenness and anxiety about this life, because that day will come upon you, and everyone on earth, as suddenly as a trap.

'When a man goes away from home he gives authority to his servants and assigns to each his work, and orders the door-keeper to keep watch. So you watch too, because you do not know when the master of the house is coming – late or at midnight, at cockcrow or dawn. He must not come unexpectedly and catch you sleeping. What I say to you, I say to everyone: "Stay awake!"'

He taught in the temple during the day, and spent his nights on the Mount of Olives. In the morning all the people would come to the temple to listen to him.

(MATTHEW 24:21–5,29–31,36,42; MARK 13:19–27,32–7; LUKE 21:25–7,34–8)

BE READY FOR THE COMING OF THE BRIDEGROOM

'The kingdom of heaven is like ten bridesmaids who went out to meet the bridegroom, taking their own lamps. Five of them were foolish and five were prudent; the foolish ones took no extra oil with them, but the prudent ones took flasks of oil with their lamps.

'The bridegroom was late, so they all became drowsy and went to sleep. But in the middle of the night the cry was raised: "The bridegroom is here; go out and meet him." So they woke up and trimmed their lamps.

'Then the foolish ones said to the others: "Give us some of your oil; our lamps are going out." But they said: "There won't be enough for all of us; you'd better go to the people who sell it and buy some for yourselves."

'While they were gone, the bridegroom arrived. The bridesmaids who were ready went in with him to the wedding feast, and the door was shut.

'Later the others arrived, and called out: "Lord, lord, open the door to us." But he answered: "I tell you truly, I don't know you."

'So keep awake, because you do not know the day or the hour.'

(MATTHEW 25:1–13)

WE MUST MAKE GOD'S GIFTS PRODUCTIVE[14]

'Ⓣhe kingdom is like a man leaving home for a time who summoned his servants and put them in charge of his possessions. Before he left he assigned five silver talents to one servant, two to another, and one to another, according to the ability of each.

'The servant who had been given five talents began at once doing business with them, and made a profit of five more. In the same way, the one who received two talents made two more. But the servant who had been given one talent dug a hole in the ground and hid his master's silver.

'After a long time, their master returned and asked for their accounts. The one he had given five talents came and said: "Master, you gave me five talents; see, I have earned five more." His master said to him: "Well done, good and faithful servant. You were faithful over a few things, so I will put you in charge of many. Come and share your master's happiness."

'Then the one he had given two talents came and said: "Master, you gave me two talents; see, I have earned two more." His master said to him: "Well done, good and faithful servant; you were faithful over a few things, so I will put you in charge of many. Come and share your master's happiness."

'Then came the one he had given one talent, who said: "Master, I knew that you are a hard man, reaping where you did not sow, and harvesting where you scattered no seed; so I was afraid and went and hid your talent in the ground. Here it is; you have it back." His master replied: "Evil and lazy servant, you knew that I reap where I did not sow, and harvest where I scattered no seed? Then you should have given my silver to the bankers, and when I came back I would have received my capital with interest."

'So take the talent from him and give it to the one with ten. Because to one who has something, more will be given and he will have plenty; but from one who has nothing, even what he has will be taken away. Throw the useless servant out into the dark, where there will be wailing and gnashing of teeth.'

(MATTHEW 25:14–30)

THE LAST JUDGEMENT

When the Son of Man comes in his glory and all the angels with him, he will sit on his throne of glory. All the nations will be assembled before him, and he will separate people from one another as a shepherd separates sheep from goats; he will place the sheep on his right and the goats on his left.

'Then the King will say to those on his right: "Come, you who are blessed by my Father, inherit the kingdom prepared for you from the foundation of the world. Because I was hungry, and you gave me food; I was thirsty, and you gave me drink. I was a stranger, and you took me in; naked, and you clothed me. I was sick, and you cared for me; I was in prison, and you came to visit me."

'Then the righteous will ask him: "Lord, when did we see you hungry and feed you, or thirsty and give you drink? When did we see you a stranger and take you in, or naked and clothe you? When did we see you sick or in prison and come to you?"

'And the king will answer them: "I tell you truly, when you did it for the least of my brothers or sisters, you did it for me."

'Then he will say to those on his left: "Leave me, accursed ones; go into the eternal fire prepared for the devil and his angels. Because I was hungry, and you did not give me food; I was thirsty, and you did not give me drink. I was a stranger, and you did not take me in; naked, and you did not clothe me; sick and in prison, and you did not visit me."

'Then they too will ask him: "Lord, when did we see you hungry or thirsty, or a stranger or naked, or sick or in prison and did not come to your help?" And he will answer: "I tell you truly, when you did not do it to one of the least of these, you did not do it to me." And they will go away into eternal punishment, but the righteous into eternal life.'

(MATTHEW 25:31–46)

JUDAS IS HIRED TO BETRAY JESUS

When Jesus had finished saying these things it was two days to Passover, the feast of unleavened bread, and he said to his disciples: 'You know that at Passover the Son of Man will be handed over to be crucified.'

The chief priests and elders and scribes of the people met at the court of the high priest Caiaphas to discuss how they could capture Jesus by stealth and kill him. But they were afraid of the people; they said: 'Not at the feast, or there may be a riot.'

Satan entered into Judas called Iscariot, one of the twelve. He went to the chief priests and captains and told them he could betray Jesus to them, and asked: 'What are you willing to give me if I deliver him to you?'

They were delighted by his offer and promised to pay him. They weighed out thirty pieces of silver, and he agreed to this amount. From then on he looked for an opportunity to hand Jesus over when no crowd was with him.

(MATTHEW 26:1–5,14–16; MARK 14:1–2,10–11;
LUKE 22:1–6)

THE LAST SUPPER

efore the Passover feast Jesus knew that his hour had come to go from this world to the Father. Having loved his own in the world, he loved them to the end.

On the first day of unleavened bread, the day when the Passover lamb was sacrificed, he told two of his disciples, Peter and John: 'Go and prepare for us to eat the Passover.'

They asked: 'Where do you want us to prepare it?' He said: 'As you go into the city, a certain man will meet you carrying a pitcher of water. Follow him into the house he enters, and tell the owner the teacher says: "My time is near. I will keep Passover at your house; where is the guest-room in which I can eat the Passover with my disciples?"

'He will show you a large upper room, all furnished. Get ready for us there.' The disciples went into the city and did as Jesus had told them; everything happened as he had said, and they prepared the Passover supper.

In the evening when the time came he arrived with the

twelve apostles. They reclined at table and he said: 'I wanted very much to eat this Passover with you before I suffer, because I tell you, I will not eat it again until it is fulfilled in the kingdom of God.'

Taking the cup, he gave thanks and said: 'Take this and share it among yourselves, because I tell you truly, I will not drink the fruit of the vine again until I drink new wine with you in the coming kingdom of my Father.'

But there was rivalry among them about who was the most important. So he said to them: 'The kings of the gentiles lord it over them, and they call those in authority benefactors. It must not be like this among you. The greatest among you must behave like the youngest, and the one in charge like a servant. Who is greater, the one at table or the one who serves? But I am among you as the one who serves.

'You are the ones who have stayed with me through all my trials, and I confer a kingdom on you as my Father conferred it on me, so that you will eat and drink at my table in my kingdom and sit on thrones to judge the twelve tribes of Israel.'

Jesus Washes His Disciples' Feet

Now that the devil had put it into the mind of Judas Iscariot, son of Simon, to betray him, Jesus – knowing that the Father had given him everything, and that he had come from God and was going to God – got up from supper, took off his clothes and put a towel round his waist. Then he put water in a basin and began to wash the feet of his disciples, and dry them with the towel he was wearing.

When Jesus came to him, Simon Peter said: 'Lord, are you washing my feet?' Jesus answered: 'You don't yet know what I am doing, but afterwards you will understand.' Peter said: 'No! You will never wash my feet.' Jesus answered: 'Unless I wash you, you have no share with me.' Then Simon Peter said: 'Lord, then wash not only my feet, but also my hands and my head.'

Jesus answered: 'One who has bathed is clean all over; he needs only to wash his feet. And most of you are clean; but not all of you.' He said this because he knew the one who was about to betray him.

When he had washed their feet and dressed himself and reclined again, he said to the disciples: 'Do you understand what I have done to you? You call me teacher and lord, and rightly; so I am. But if I, your lord and teacher, have washed your feet, you too must wash one another's feet. I have given you an example so that you will do as I have done to you. Truly I tell you, a servant is not greater than his master, nor an apostle than the one who sends him.

'Once you understand these things, you will be blessed for doing them. But I am not speaking of all of you; I know whom I chose in fulfilment of the text "One who has eaten my bread lifted his heel against me." I am telling you this before it happens, so that when it happens you will believe that I AM.

'I assure you, whoever receives someone I send receives me, and whoever receives me receives the one who sent me.'

(MATTHEW 26:17–20,29; MARK 14:12–17,25;

LUKE 22:7–18,24–30; JOHN 13:1–20)

Judas Leaves to Betray Jesus

After saying these things Jesus was troubled in spirit, and while they were reclining and eating he told them the reason: 'In all truth I tell you, one of you is going to betray me; one who is eating with me.'

The disciples looked at one another, at a loss to know who he meant. They were disturbed, and began to say to him one by one: 'Not I, Lord, surely?'

But Jesus said: 'Look, next to my hand on the table is the hand of the one who will betray me – one of you twelve, dipping his hand in the same dish with me. The Son of Man is indeed going to his fate, just as scripture has foretold; but woe to the man by whom he is betrayed! Better for him if he had never been born.'

Then the disciples began to argue about which of them might do such a thing. The one Jesus loved was reclining next to him, so Simon Peter nodded to him and said: 'Ask him who he means.' He leaned back against Jesus' breast and asked him: 'Lord, who is it?'

Jesus answered: 'The one to whom I give the piece of bread I dip.' He dipped the bread and gave it to Judas, son of Simon Iscariot.

Judas, the one who would betray Jesus, had also said to him: 'Surely not I, Lord?' Jesus answered: 'As you have said.'

After he swallowed the bread, Satan entered into him. Jesus said to him: 'Be quick about what you are doing,' and he went out at once. Night had come.

None of those reclining knew what Jesus had told him to do. Since Judas kept the purse, some thought Jesus had told him to buy things they needed for the feast, or to give something to the poor.

When Judas was gone, Jesus said: 'Now has the Son of Man been glorified, and God has been glorified in him. God will glorify him in himself, and will glorify him at once.

'Children, I will be with you only a little longer. You will look for me, but I tell you now what I told the Jews: where I am going, you cannot come. A new commandment I give you, that as I have loved you, you too must love one another. By your love for one another everyone will know that you are my disciples.'

(MATTHEW 26:21–5; MARK 14:18–21;
LUKE 22:21–3; JOHN 13:21–35)

Jesus Offers His Coming Sacrifice to His Father

While they were at supper on the night he was betrayed, the Lord Jesus took bread, gave thanks, broke it and gave it to the disciples saying: 'Take and eat; this is my body, sacrificed for your sake. Do this in memory of me.'

In the same way, after the supper, he took the cup, gave thanks and gave it to them saying: 'Drink from this, all of you; this cup is my blood of the new covenant, shed for you and for many for the forgiveness of sins. Whenever you drink it, drink it in memory of me.' And they all drank from it.

(MATTHEW 26:26–8; MARK 14:22–4;
LUKE 22:19–20; 1 CORINTHIANS 11:23B–25)

He Foretells Peter's Denials

Then Jesus said to them: 'Tonight you will all desert me, because it has been written: "I will strike the shepherd, and the sheep of the flock will be scattered." But after I am raised from death I will go ahead of you to Galilee.

'Simon, listen: Satan has coveted the chance to sift you all like wheat. But I have prayed for you, Simon, that your faith may not fail, and that when you have turned back to me you will confirm your brothers.'

Simon Peter said: 'Lord, where are you going?' Jesus answered: 'Where I am going, you cannot follow me now, but you will follow later.'

Peter replied: 'Lord, why can't I follow you now? Even if everyone deserts you, I never will. I am ready to go to prison with you, or even to death; I will lay down my life for you.'

Jesus answered: 'You will lay down your life for me? Peter, I tell you truly, the cock will not crow twice tonight before you deny three times that you know me.' But Peter protested vehemently: 'Even if I must die with you, I will never deny you'; and all the others said the same.

Then Jesus said to them: 'When I sent you out without purse or bag or spare sandals, were you short of anything?' They said: 'No, nothing.' He went on: 'But now take a purse, if you have it, and a bag as well; and if you have no sword, sell your cloak and buy one, because I tell you, this prophecy about me has to be fulfilled: "He was counted among the lawless." What was foretold about me is coming true.'

They said: 'Look, Lord, here are two swords.' He said: 'That is enough.'

(MATTHEW 26:31–5; MARK 14:27–31; LUKE
22:31–8; JOHN 13:36–8)

Jesus Goes to Prepare a Home for Us and Sends the Spirit to Guide Us

'Let your hearts not be troubled; you trust in God, so trust me. In my Father's house there are many dwellings; if not, I would have told you. I am going to prepare a place for you, and when I have, I will come back to fetch you so that where I am, you can be with me. In any case, you know the way.'

Thomas said: 'Lord, we don't know where you're going, so how can we know the way?' Jesus answered: 'I am the way, and the truth, and the life; no one comes to the Father except through me. If you had known who I was, you would have known my Father too; now you do know him, and have seen him.'

Philip said: 'Lord, show us the Father and we will be satisfied.' Jesus answered: 'Philip, have I been with you all this time and you still don't know who I am? Whoever has seen me has seen the Father; so how can you say: "Show us the Father"? Don't you believe that I am in the Father and the Father is in me?

'Believe it, then, on the evidence of the miracles you have seen; it is the Father living in me who works his miracles. I do not say what I say to you of my own accord. And I assure you, if anyone believes in me, he will do the miracles I do – even greater miracles, because I am going to the Father and whatever you ask in my name I will do, so that the Father may be glorified in the Son.

'If you love me you will keep my commandments, and I will ask the Father to give you another helper and guide to be with you for ever: the Spirit of Truth, whom the world cannot accept because it does not see him or know him. But you will know him, because he will stay with you; he will be in you.

'I will not leave you orphans; I am coming to you. In a little while the world will see me no more, but you will see me again, and because I am alive you also will live. On that day you will know that I am in my Father, and you in me, and I in you.

'Those who know and keep my commandments are the ones who love me; and whoever loves me will be loved by my Father, and I will love him and reveal myself to him.'

Jude (not Judas Iscariot) said: 'Lord, why will you reveal yourself only to us, and not to the world?' Jesus answered: 'If anyone loves me he will do as I have taught you, and my Father will love him and we will come to him and make our home with him. One who does not love me does not do what I teach. And what I have taught you is not my own teaching, but that of the Father who sent me.

'I have told you these things while I was with you. But the Holy Spirit, the helper and guide the Father will send in my name, will teach you everything and remind you of everything I have told you.

'I leave you peace; I give you my own peace, not what the world offers. Let your hearts not be troubled or afraid. You have heard me say that I am going, and that I will come to you; if you loved me, you would have rejoiced that I am going to the Father, because he is greater[15] than I.

'I have told you about this before it happens so that when it happens you will believe me. I have no time to tell you much more, because the ruler of the world is coming. He has no power over me, but I must do what the Father has command-ed so that the world will know that I love him.

'Get up; we must leave here.'

(JOHN 14:1–31)

He is the Vine, We Are the Branches

'I am the true vine, and my Father is the vinedresser. Every branch in me that does not bear fruit he cuts away, and he prunes other branches to make them bear more. You have already been pruned by the things I have taught you; so remain in me, and I will remain in you. A branch cannot bear fruit unless it remains part of the vine; neither can you unless you remain in me.

'I am the vine and you are the branches. If you remain in me and I in you, you will bear much fruit, but cut off from me you can do nothing. Unless someone remains in me, he is like a branch that is thrown away; he withers and dies. Branches like that are collected and thrown on the fire.

'But if you remain in me and hold fast to what I have taught you, you may ask whatever you wish and it will be done for you. This is what gives glory to my Father: that you are my dis-ciples and bear much fruit.'

(JOHN 15:1–8)

Jesus' Own Commandment

'As the Father has loved me, I have loved you: remain in my love. If you keep my commandments you will remain in my love, just as I have kept the commandments of my Father and remain in his love.

'I have told you these things so that my joy may be in you and your joy may be full. This is my commandment, that you love one another as I loved you; no one has greater love than this, that he lay down his life for his friends.

'You are my friends if you do what I command you. I no longer call you servants, because a servant does not know what his master does; I call you friends, because I have made known to you everything I learned from my Father.

'You did not choose me; I chose you, and commissioned you to go and bear fruit that will last; then the Father will give you whatever you ask in my name.

'The reason I tell you to do these things is so that you will love one another.'

(JOHN 15:9–17)

Why the World Hates Christians

'If the world hates you, remember that it hated me before you. If you belonged to the world, the world would have loved you as its own. But you do not belong to the world; I chose you out of the world, and that is why it hates you.

'Remember what I told you: "A servant is not greater than his master." If they have persecuted me, they will persecute you too; if they have accepted what I taught, they will accept what you teach. They will do all these things to you on

account of my name because they do not know the one who
sent me.

'If I had not come and taught them, they would not have
been guilty of their sin; but now they cannot plead ignorance
of it. Whoever hates me hates my Father too. If I had not done
miracles among them which no man ever did, they would not
have been guilty of sin; but now, though they saw them, they
have hated both me and my Father. In this way the text in their
law is being fulfilled: "They hated me without cause."

'When the helper and guide comes whom I will send to you
from the Father – the Spirit of Truth, who proceeds from the
Father – he will testify in my favour. You are also my witnesses, because you were with me from the beginning.

'I have told you these things so that your faith will not be
brought down. They will expel you from the synagogue, and a
time will come when anyone who kills you will think he is
serving God; they will do these things because they know neither the Father nor me. But I have warned you so that when the
time comes, you will remember that I told you. I did not tell
you these things at first, because I was with you; but now I am
going to the one who sent me.'

(JOHN 15:18–27; 16:1–5A)

The Spirit of Truth Guides Us into the Whole Truth

'None of you asks me now where I am going, but because I
have said these things to you, grief has filled your hearts. But I
tell you the truth: it is better for you that I go. If I did not go,
the helper and guide would not come to you; but when I go, I
will send him to you.

'When he comes he will show the world how wrong it was about sin, and righteousness, and judgement: about its own sin, because people did not believe in me; about my righteousness, because I am going to the Father and you will no longer see me; and about who deserved judgement, because it is the ruler of this world that has been condemned.

'There are many more things I could tell you, but they would be too much for you now. When the Spirit of Truth comes he will guide you into the whole truth. He will not teach a doctrine of his own, but will tell you what he has heard, and reveal to you what must still become known. He will glorify me, because he will receive what is mine and declare it to you. I say this because everything the Father has is mine.'

(JOHN 16:5B–15)

Jesus' Coming Death and Resurrection

'In a little while you will see me no more; a little while longer, and you will see me again.'

Some of his disciples asked one another: 'What does he mean by this, and by saying: "Because I am going to the Father"? What is this "little while"? We don't understand.'

Jesus knew they wanted to question him and said: 'Are you discussing why I said: "In a little while you will see me no more; a little while longer, and you will see me again"? I tell you most truly, you will weep and lament while the world rejoices; you will grieve, but your grief will turn into joy.

'When her time comes to give birth, a woman suffers pain, but later she forgets the pain for joy that a child has been born into the world. You are grieving already, but I will see you again and your hearts will rejoice, and that joy no one will take away. On that day you will not ask me any questions.

'Truly I assure you, whatever you ask the Father in my name he will give you. Till now you have not asked anything in my name; ask, and you will receive, so that your joy may be full.'

(JOHN 16:16–24)

No More Parables: Time to Speak Plainly

'I have been telling you these things in parables, but the time is coming when I will no longer speak this way, and will tell you plainly and clearly about the Father. Then you will pray in my name. I do not say I will ask the Father on your behalf, because the Father himself loves you for having loved me, and for believing that I came from him. I came out of the Father and into the world, and now I am leaving the world and going to the Father.'

His disciples said: 'See, now you are talking plainly, not in parables. Now we know that you know everything, and do not need anyone to question you; by this we believe that you came forth from God.'

Jesus answered: 'Do you believe now? Listen, the time is coming – in fact it is here – when you will run for your own homes and leave me alone; except that I am never alone, because the Father is with me.

'I have said these things to you so that you may have peace in me. In the world you will have suffering, but have courage: I have overcome the world.'

(JOHN 16:25–33)

Jesus' Prayer for Us to His Father

After saying these things Jesus raised his eyes to heaven and said: 'Father, the time has come. Give glory to your Son so that he will give glory to you. You have given him authority over all mankind, to give eternal life to those you have given him; and this is eternal life: to know you, the only true God, and Jesus Christ whom you have sent.

'I have given glory to you on earth and finished the work you gave me to do. Now, Father, give me again the glory I had with you before the world existed.

'I have made you known to those you gave me from the world. They were yours and you gave them to me, and they have been faithful to your message. They know now that all you have given me comes from you, because I gave them the message you gave me, and they have accepted it. They know that I came from you; they believe that you sent me.

'I make this prayer not for the world, but for those you have given me, since they are yours. Everything of mine is yours and everything of yours is mine, and I have been glorified in them. I am no longer in the world; they are in the world, but I am coming to you.

'Holy Father, keep them true to your name which you have given to me, so that they may be one as we are one. While I was with them, I kept them faithful; I watched over them so that none was lost, except the one who deserved to be lost in fulfilment of scripture. But now that I am coming to you, I say these things in the world to fill them with my joy.

'I have passed on your message to them, and the world hated them because they do not belong to the world any more than I do. I do not ask you to take them out of the world, but to protect them from the evil one. Consecrate them by the truth of your word. As you sent me into the world, I sent them into the world; and on their behalf I consecrate myself, so that they may be consecrated in truth.

'I pray not only for these, but for all who will come to believe in me through their teaching. Father, may they all be one, as you are in me and I am in you; may they be one in us, so that the world will believe that you sent me. I have shared with them the glory you have given me to make them one as we are one, I in them and you in me; to make them so completely one that the world will know that you sent me, and that you have loved them as you loved me.

'Father, may those you have given me be with me where I am to see the glory you gave me, because you loved me before the foundation of the world. Righteous Father, the world did not know you; but I know you, and these know that you have sent me. I have made you known and I will make you known to them, so that your love for me may be in them, and that I may be in them.'

(JOHN 17)

The Agony in the Garden

When Jesus had said this and they had sung a hymn, he and his disciples went out across the Kedron river to the Mount of Olives, as he often did, to a garden on a piece of land called Gethsemane. Then he said to them: 'Sit here while I go over there to pray.' He took with him Peter and James and John.

He began to feel amazement and anguish, and said to them: 'My soul is grieved to death. Stay here and keep awake with me, and pray that you will not be put to the test.'

Going a stone's throw further, he prostrated himself face to the ground and prayed that if possible this hour might pass him by: 'Abba, my Father, everything is possible to you; if you will, take this cup away from me. Nevertheless, not what I wish, but your will be done.'

An angel from heaven appeared to him, strengthening him. In agony he prayed more earnestly, and his sweat became like drops of blood falling on the ground.

Then, rising from prayer, he came to the disciples and found them asleep from grief. He said: 'Simon, are you asleep?' and to the others: 'Why are you sleeping? Couldn't you keep awake with me for one hour? Get up, stay awake and pray that you will not be tested. The spirit may be eager, but the flesh is weak.'

A second time he went away and prayed in the same words: 'My Father, if this cup cannot pass unless I drink it, your will be done.'

Again he came to the disciples and found them sleeping. Their eyes were getting heavy, and they didn't know how to answer him. Leaving them again he went to pray a third time, still in the same words.

Then he came back to the disciples and said: 'Still sleeping? You've rested enough; the time has come, the Son of Man has been betrayed into the hands of sinners. Get up, let us go; the traitor is near.'

Since Judas who betrayed him was one of the twelve, he knew where Jesus and his disciples often went. While Jesus was still speaking he arrived with representatives of the chief priests, scribes, Pharisees and elders of the people, a detachment of guards, and a crowd with lanterns and torches, swords and clubs.

The traitor had arranged to give them a sign: 'The one I kiss, he is the man; make him secure and take him away.' Jesus, knowing everything that was going to happen to him, stepped forward and asked: 'Who are you looking for?' They answered: 'Jesus the Nazarene.' He told them: 'I am he.' Judas the betrayer was standing with them, but when Jesus said: 'I am he,' they drew back and fell to the ground.

He asked them again: 'Who are you looking for?' When they said again: 'Jesus the Nazarene,' he said: 'I have told you I am he. If you are looking for me, let these others go.' In this way he fulfilled what he had said: 'I watched over those you have given me so that none was lost.'

Then Judas came to Jesus and said: 'Hail, Rabbi,' and kissed him fervently. Jesus answered: 'Judas, friend, do you betray the Son of Man with a kiss? Do what you have come here to do.' Then others came forward, laid hands on Jesus and seized him.

Some who stood near saw what would happen and said: 'Lord, shall we strike with a sword?' Simon Peter had one; he drew it and struck a servant of the high priest named Malchus, cutting off his right ear. But Jesus said: 'Let them have their way for now.' Touching the servant's ear, he healed him.

Then he said to Peter: 'Put your sword back in the scabbard; those who take up the sword will perish by a sword. Do you think I will not drink the cup that the Father has given me?

Don't you realize that I could ask my Father to send more than twelve legions of angels to my defence? But then how would the scriptures be fulfilled which say that these things must happen?'

To the chief priests, captains of the temple guard and elders, and to the crowd that was coming upon him, Jesus said: 'Did you come out to arrest me with swords and clubs, as if I were a robber? When I sat among you teaching in the temple every day, you didn't lay a hand on me to arrest me; but this is your hour, and the hour of the prince of darkness. Everything that is happening fulfils the writings of the prophets.'

Then all the disciples left him and ran away. The others seized a young man who had been with Jesus and was wearing only a linen cloth over his body, but he let go of the cloth and fled naked. Then the tribune and soldiers and the temple guard took hold of Jesus and bound him.

MATTHEW 26:30,36–56; MARK 14:26,32–52;

LUKE 22:39–53; JOHN 18:1–12)

THE PASSION AND DEATH OF JESUS

Jesus Is Judged a Blasphemer and Found Worthy of Death
They led Jesus away and brought him into the house of the high priest. First they took him to Annas, the father-in-law of Caiaphas who was high priest that year. It was Caiaphas who had advised the Jews that it was expedient for one man to die for the sake of the people.

The high priest[16] interrogated Jesus about his disciples and what he had taught them. But Jesus answered: 'I have spoken openly to everyone; I always taught in a synagogue or in the temple, where all the Jews come together. I have taught nothing in secret, so why question me? Ask those who listened to me what I taught them; they know what I said.'

At this, one of the guards standing by slapped him in the face and said: 'Is that how you answer the high priest?' Jesus answered: 'If I said anything wrong, say what it was; if I answered rightly, why hit me?'

So Annas sent him bound to Caiaphas, in whose house all the chief priests, scribes and elders had assembled. The priests and the sanhedrin were looking for evidence against Jesus so that they could condemn him to death, but they could not find any. Many false witnesses came forward and testified against him, but their testimonies did not agree.

Eventually two men came forward to give false evidence. They said: 'We heard this man say: "I will demolish this man-made temple of God, and in three days I will raise another not built by men."' But their testimonies did not agree either.

So standing up in the middle, the high priest asked Jesus: 'Have you no answer to what these men testify against you?' But Jesus remained silent. Again the high priest questioned him and said: 'I adjure you by the living God that you tell us whether you are the Messiah, the Son of the blessed God.'

Then Jesus answered: 'I am as you have said. And I tell you, one day you will see the Son of Man sitting on the right of the Power, and coming on the clouds of heaven.'

At this the high priest tore his tunic and said: 'He has blasphemed. What need have we of witnesses now? You have all

heard the blasphemy; what is your opinion?' And they all condemned him as deserving of death.

Then the guards in charge of him made fun of him. Some
began to spit in his face, and to slap and beat him and treat him
with violence. They blindfolded him and said: 'Prophesy to us,
Messiah; tell us who hit you!' And they spoke many other blasphemies against him

(MATTHEW 26:57,59–68; MARK 14:53,55–65;
LUKE 22:54A,63–5; JOHN 18:13–14,19–24)

Peter Swears He Never Knew Jesus

Simon Peter and another disciple had followed Jesus at a
distance to the court of the high priest. This disciple was
known to the high priest and went into the court with Jesus,
while Peter stood at the door outside.

It was cold, so the servants and guards made a fire in the
courtyard and stood or sat around it. The other disciple came
out, spoke to one of the high priest's maids – the doorkeeper –
and brought Simon Peter into the courtyard. He joined the others, warming himself at the bright fire and waiting to see the
end.

When the doorkeeper saw him by the light of the fire, she
looked at him intently; then she came to him and said: 'You're
not one of this man's disciples, are you? Yes, you were also
with Jesus, the Galilean from Nazareth!' And she told the
others: 'This man was with him.'

But he denied it in front of everyone, saying: 'Woman, I was
not; I don't know what you mean. I don't know what you're
talking about; I don't know the man.' And he went outside to

the porch. But another maid saw him going and began telling the bystanders on the porch: 'This man was with Jesus the Nazarene; he's one of them.' So they said to him: 'Surely you're not one of his disciples?' And soon someone said: 'Yes, you are one of them.' Again Peter denied it: 'Man, I am not!' And with an oath he said: 'I don't know the man.'

But soon the bystanders were telling Peter: 'You must be one of them. You're a Galilean; your accent proves it,' and an hour later one man was still insisting: 'He must have been with him; he is certainly a Galilean.' And one of the high priest's servants, a relative of the man whose ear Peter cut off, said: 'Didn't I see you in the garden with him?' Then Peter began to curse and swear and say: 'Man, I don't know what you mean; I don't know the man you are talking about.'

Just then, while he was speaking, a cock crew for the second time, and Jesus turned and looked at him. Then Peter remembered how the Lord had said that before a cock crew twice that morning, he would deny him three times.

Thinking of that, he went outside and wept bitterly.

(MATTHEW 26:58,69–75; MARK 14:54,66–72;
LUKE 22:54B,55–62; JOHN 18:15–18,25–7)

The Official Morning Session of the Sanhedrin

Early in the morning, the whole body of chief priests was assembled in council with the elders of the people, the scribes and all the sanhedrin, to discuss the fate of Jesus so that they could put him to death.

He was brought before them and ordered: 'If you are the Messiah, tell us.'

He answered: 'If I tell you, you will not believe it, and if I question you, you will not answer. But from now on the Son of Man will be sitting at the right of the power of God.'

They all said: 'Then you are the Son of God?'

He answered: 'As you say; I AM.'

And they said: 'Why do we still need witnesses? We have heard for ourselves, from his own mouth.'

(MATTHEW 27:1; MARK 15:1A; LUKE 22:66–71)

Judas Hangs Himself

When Judas who betrayed Jesus knew that he had been condemned, he repented and returned the thirty pieces of silver to the chief priests and elders, saying: 'I have sinned by betraying innocent blood.'

But they said: 'What is that to us? You decide what to do with the money.' So he threw it down in the temple, and went away and hanged himself.

The priests took the pieces of silver, but said: 'It is not lawful to put them into the treasury, since they are the price of blood.' They debated what they should do and then used them to buy the potter's field as a burial place for foreigners. That is why it is called Field of Blood to this day.

In this way what had been foretold through the prophet Jeremiah was fulfilled: 'They took the thirty pieces of silver, the price set on the valued one by the sons of Israel, and gave them for the potter's field, as the Lord directed me.'

(MATTHEW 27:3–10)

Jesus Is Brought before Pilate

Then all of them stood up, and when Jesus had been bound, they led him from the house of Caiaphas to the praetorium and delivered him to Pilate the governor. It was still early, and they did not defile themselves by going into the praetorium, since they were to eat the Passover. So Pilate came out to them and Jesus stood before him. The governor said: 'What accusation do you bring against this man?'

Then they began to accuse Jesus, saying: 'If this man were not a criminal, we would not have delivered him to you. We found him leading our nation astray by forbidding payment of tribute to Caesar, and claiming to be the Christ, a king.'

So Pilate said to them: 'Take him and judge him according to your own law.' But the Jews answered: 'We are not allowed to execute anyone', fulfilling what Jesus had said about the kind of death he would die.

So Pilate went back into the praetorium and summoned Jesus. The governor questioned him, saying: 'Are you the king of the Jews?'

Jesus answered: 'As you say. But do you ask this of your own accord, or have others told you about me?'

Pilate answered: 'Am I a Jew? Your nation and chief priests handed you over to me. What have you done?'

Jesus answered: 'My kingdom is not of this world. If it were, my soldiers would have fought against surrendering me to the Jews; but my kingdom is not from here.'

Then Pilate said to him: 'So you really are a king?' Jesus answered: 'You say I am a king. I was born into the world for this: to bear witness to the truth; and everyone who belongs to the truth listens to my voice.'

Pilate responded: 'What is truth?'

Having said this, he went out to the Jews again and told the chief priests and the crowd: 'I do not find this man guilty of any crime.' But the chief priests and elders insisted, saying: 'All over Judaea he stirs up the people by his teaching, from Galilee to here.' And they brought several more accusations against him; but Jesus made no answer.

So Pilate spoke to him again, saying: 'Don't you hear all the accusations they bring against you? Aren't you going to answer any of them?' But Jesus answered not a word, and the governor was amazed.

Then, having heard Galilee mentioned, Pilate asked if the man was a Galilean. When he discovered that he came under Herod's jurisdiction, he sent him to Herod, who was also in Jerusalem at the time. Herod was delighted to see Jesus; he had heard about him, and had wanted for a long time to see him, hoping to see him work some miracle.

He questioned him at length, but Jesus gave him no answer, though the chief priests and scribes were also there and accused him vehemently. So Herod and his soldiers began to despise and ridicule Jesus. Then they put a splendid cloak on him and sent him back to Pilate. Herod and Pilate, who had been enemies, became friends that very day.

Pilate then called together the chief priests, the leaders and the people and said to them: 'You brought this man to me on the grounds that he was leading the people astray. I have examined him in your presence and found nothing that would make him guilty of the charges you have brought against him. Neither did Herod; that is why he sent him back to us. Since he has done nothing that deserves the death penalty, I will punish him and then release him.'

(MATTHEW 27:2,11–14; MARK 15:1B,2–5;
LUKE 23:1–16; JOHN 18:28–38)

'Crucify Him!'

At Passover it was the custom for the Jews to petition the governor to release a prisoner of their choice, so a crowd gathered and went to Pilate to ask him to do what was customary.

In the jail there was a notorious robber named Barabbas; during an insurrection in the city he had been arrested together with some insurgents who had committed murder. So Pilate asked them: 'Who do you want me to release for you: Barabbas, or Jesus called the Messiah, the King of the Jews?'

He knew that the chief priests had handed Jesus over out of envy. And while he was on the judgement seat, his wife sent him a message: 'Have nothing to do with punishing that just man. I suffered many things today in a dream because of him.'

But the chief priests and the elders had stirred up the crowd to ask him to release Barabbas and put Jesus to death; so when the governor asked them which of the two they wanted him to release, the whole crowd shouted: 'Not this man; take him away! Release Barabbas!'

Wanting to release Jesus, Pilate called out to the crowd: 'What then shall I do with Jesus, the one you call Messiah and

King of the Jews?' And they all shouted: 'Crucify him, crucify him!'

He spoke to them a third time: 'Why, what has this man done wrong? I found no reason to put him to death, so I will punish him and then release him.' But they shouted all the louder: 'Crucify him!'

When Pilate saw he could not persuade them and that there was likely to be a riot, their voices prevailed. He decided to give them their way and granted what they asked; he released the man who had been jailed for insurrection and murder and gave Jesus up to their will.

Asking for water, he washed his hands in front of the crowd, saying: 'I am innocent of this man's blood: it is your responsibility.' And all the people answered: 'His blood be on us, and on our children.' Then Pilate released Barabbas for them.

(MATTHEW 27:15–26A; MARK 15:6–15A;
LUKE 23:18–25; JOHN 18:39–40)

Jesus Scourged and Crowned with Thorns

So the governor Pilate had Jesus scourged and then handed him over to be crucified. The soldiers led him into the praetorium and assembled the whole cohort in front of him. They stripped him naked and threw a purple cloak around him; they plaited a wreath of thorns and put it on his head for a crown, with a reed in his right hand. They came up to salute him, genuflecting in mock homage and saying: 'Hail, king of the Jews!' Then they beat him, hit his head with the reed, and spat at him.

(MATTHEW 27:26B–30; MARK 15:15B–19;
JOHN 19:1–3)

Pilate's Last Stand

Pilate went outside again and said: 'See, I bring him out to you to let you know that I do not find him guilty of any crime.' Jesus came out wearing the crown of thorns and the purple cloak, and Pilate said: 'Look, this is the man.' But when the chief priests and their attendants saw him, they shouted: 'Crucify him, crucify him!'

Pilate answered: 'You take him and crucify him; I find him guilty of no crime.' The Jews replied: 'We have a law, and according to that law he ought to die, because he claimed to be the Son of God.'

When Pilate heard that, he was even more afraid. He went into the praetorium again and asked Jesus: 'Where do you come from?' But Jesus gave him no answer. Pilate said: 'Are you refusing to speak to me? Don't you know that I have authority to release you or to crucify you?' Jesus answered: 'You would have no authority over me unless it were given you from above; so the one who gave me up to you has committed the greater sin.'

After this Pilate tried again to release him. But the Jews shouted: 'If you release this man, you are no friend of Caesar; anyone who claims to be a king opposes himself to Caesar.'

When Pilate heard this he brought Jesus out again and sat on a judgement seat at the place called the Pavement (in Hebrew, Gabbatha). It was now the morning[17] of the preparation day of Passover. He said to the Jews: 'Look, here is your king.' They shouted: 'Take him away, take him away, crucify him!' Pilate said: 'Shall I crucify your king?' The chief priests answered: 'We have no king but Caesar.'

(JOHN 19:4–15)

Jesus Carries His Cross to Calvary

So they led Jesus away to crucify him and he went out carrying his cross. But on the way they stopped a man coming in from the country – a Cyrenian named Simon, the father of Alexander and Rufus – and laid the cross on him, and made him carry it behind Jesus.

A large crowd followed him, including some women who mourned and lamented him. Jesus turned to them and said: 'Daughters of Jerusalem, do not weep for me; weep rather for yourselves and your children, because a time is coming when people will say: "Blessed are the barren, the wombs which never bore and breasts which were never sucked." Then they will begin to say to the mountains, "Fall on us," and to the hills, "Cover us."

'If they do these things to a tree full of sap, what will become of a dry one?'

There were also two criminals who were to be crucified with him.

(MATTHEW 27:31B–32; MARK 15:20B–21;
LUKE 23:26–32; JOHN 19:16B–17A)

Jesus Crucified between Two Robbers

They brought him to the place called Golgotha, meaning skull. They offered him wine mixed with gall and myrrh which he tasted, but would not drink. It was now nine in the morning.

They crucified him there, and the two robbers on either side of him. And Jesus said: 'Father, forgive them; they do not know what they are doing.'

Pilate wrote the accusation against him as a title which they fastened to the cross above his head: 'This is Jesus of Nazareth, the King of the Jews.' Many of the Jews read it; it was written in Hebrew, Latin and Greek, and the place where Jesus was crucified was near the city.

So the chief priests of the Jews complained to Pilate: 'Do not write, "The King of the Jews," but, "This man said, 'I am the King of the Jews.'"'

But Pilate answered: 'What I have written, I have written.'

(MATTHEW 27:33–35A,37; MARK 15:22–24A,26–7;
LUKE 23:33–34A,38; JOHN 19:17B–22)

The Soldiers Draw Lots for His Clothes

When the soldiers had crucified Jesus they took his clothes and divided them in four, one part for each. But his tunic was seamless, woven in one piece from the top, so they said: 'Let's not tear it; let's throw lots to decide who will have it.'

They did, and so the scripture was fulfilled: 'They divide my garments among them, and throw lots for my clothes'; this is just what the soldiers did. Then they sat down there and guarded him.

(MATTHEW 27:35B–36; MARK 15:24B; LUKE 23:34B;
JOHN 19:23–4)

Jesus Is Mocked

As some stood watching, passers-by blasphemed him, shaking their heads and saying: 'You were going to demolish the temple and rebuild it in three days! If you are the Son of God, save yourself; come down from the cross.'

The chief priests, scribes and elders also ridiculed him, saying: 'He saved others, but can't save himself! Isn't he the Messiah, God's chosen one, the King of Israel? Let him save himself; let him come down from the cross now! When we see that, we'll believe in him. He trusted in God, so let God rescue him now, if he wants him; after all, he said: "I am the Son of God."'

Soldiers, too, went up to him and taunted him, offering him vinegar and saying: 'Save yourself, if you are the King of the Jews!' Even the robbers crucified with him reproached him; one of them blasphemed him, saying: 'You're the Messiah, aren't you? Save yourself, and us!'

But the other rebuked him: 'Have you no fear even of God? You got the same sentence he did, and we deserve it; we are being punished for what we did, but this man has done nothing wrong.' And he said: 'Jesus, remember me when you come into your kingdom.'

Jesus said to him: 'Truly I tell you, today you will be with me in paradise.'

(MATTHEW 27:39–44; MARK 15:29–32; LUKE 23:35–7,39–43)

Mary the Mother of Jesus and His Brethren

Standing by the cross of Jesus were his mother, her sister Mary the wife of Cleopas, and Mary Magdalene.

When Jesus saw the disciple he loved standing with his mother, he said to her: 'Woman, this is your son'; and to the disciple: 'This is your mother.'

From that hour, the disciple took her into his own home.

(JOHN 19:25–7)

Jesus Appeals to Prophecy, Fulfils it, and Dies

About noon the sun was darkened, and the whole country was in darkness until three o'clock. Then Jesus cried out in a loud voice: *Eli, Eli, lema shebaqtani?* 'My God, my God, why have you forsaken me?'[18]

Some of the bystanders said: 'Listen, he's calling on Elijah.'

Knowing that everything had now been completed, Jesus said in fulfilment of scripture: 'I am thirsty.' There was a jar full of vinegar there, so one of them ran at once and filled a sponge with it, put it on a stick[19] and lifted it to his mouth. But the others were saying: 'Let's wait and see if Elijah comes to take him down and save him.'

When Jesus had taken the vinegar, he said: 'It is finished.' Then he cried out with a loud voice: 'Father, into your hands I commit my spirit!' And bowing his head, he breathed his last.

The veil of the temple was torn down the middle from top to bottom. The earth was shaken, rocks were split, and tombs were opened; the bodies of many saints who had fallen asleep were raised to life, and after the resurrection of Jesus they came out of their tombs and entered the holy city, appearing to many people.

The centurion who had watched how Jesus died gave glory to God and said: 'This man truly is righteous.' And the guards under him, terrified by the earthquake and all they had seen, said: 'This man really was a son of God.' Those in the crowd who had gathered to watch, and saw what happened, went home beating their breasts.

The friends of Jesus watched everything from a distance, including many women disciples who had served him in

Galilee and on the way to Jerusalem. Among them were Mary Magdalene, Mary the mother of James the younger and of Joses, and Salome, and the mother of the sons of Zebedee.

(MATTHEW 27:45–56; MARK 15:33–41; LUKE
23:44–9; JOHN 19:28–30)

The Soldiers Make Sure He Is Dead

Since it was preparation day, the eve of the sabbath – and that sabbath was one of special solemnity – the Jews asked Pilate to have the legs broken and the bodies taken away so that they would not remain on the crosses.

The soldiers came and broke the legs of the two who were crucified with Jesus. But when they came to him and saw he was already dead, they did not break his legs. Instead, one of the soldiers pierced his side with his lance, and immediately blood and water came out. The one who saw this has testified so that you too may believe.

His testimony is true, and he knows he speaks the truth, because these things happened to fulfil the scripture 'Not a bone of his shall be broken'; and again, another text says: 'They will look at the one they have pierced.'

(MARK 15:42B; JOHN 19:31–7)

The Body of Jesus Is Laid in the Tomb

As evening came a man named Joseph plucked up courage and went to Pilate to ask for the body of Jesus. Joseph, from the Jewish town of Arimathaea, was a good and righteous man who looked forward to the kingdom of God; he was also a rich and respected member of the sanhedrin, though he had not supported their action. In fact he was a disciple of Jesus, but secretly for fear of the Jews.

Pilate was surprised to hear that Jesus was already dead, and sent for the centurion to ask how long ago he had died. After the centurion told him, he granted Joseph's request and ordered that the body be given to him.

So Joseph, and with him Nicodemus – the one who had at first come to Jesus by night – came and took his body down from the cross. Joseph had bought a clean sheet of unused linen; Nicodemus brought about a hundred pounds of mixed myrrh and aloes. They wrapped the body of Jesus in the linen with the spices, according to the burial custom of the Jews.

Where he was crucified there was a garden, and in it a new tomb which Joseph had dug out of rock for himself, in which no one had yet been laid. Because it was near, and because of the Jewish preparation day, they laid Jesus in it and rolled a great stone across the entrance; then they left.

Of the women who had come with him from Galilee, Mary Magdalene and the other Mary, the mother of Joses, had followed and were sitting opposite the tomb. They saw how his body was laid in it, and went away to prepare spices and ointment.

(MATTHEW 27:57–61; MARK 15:42A,43–7; LUKE
23:50–56A; JOHN 19:38–42)

The Tomb Is Sealed and Guarded

On the next day, the sabbath which followed that preparation day, they rested in obedience to the commandment. But the chief priests and Pharisees went to Pilate in a body and said: 'Sir, we have remembered that while he was alive, that deceiver said:

"After three days I will be raised from death." You must order that the tomb be made secure till the third day, or his disciples may come and steal him and tell the people he was raised from the dead; and then the last deception will be worse than the first.'

Pilate said to them: 'You have a guard. Go and make the tomb as secure as you know how.' So they went with the guard and secured it, putting a seal on the stone.

(MATTHEW 27:62–6; LUKE 23:56B)

THE RESURRECTION OF JESUS

The Women Find Angels in the Empty Tomb

Very early on Sunday while it was still dark, just as the sun appeared and the sabbath ended, Mary Magdalene, Salome and Mary the mother of James set out for the tomb with spices they had bought and prepared to anoint the body of Jesus.

Suddenly the earth shook violently as an angel of the Lord came down from heaven, rolled away the stone, and sat on it. His appearance was like lightning, and his dress white as snow. The guards were shaken with fear and became like dead men.

The women had been asking one another: 'Who will roll away the stone for us from the opening of the tomb?' Now, looking up, they saw the great stone already rolled back; but when they went into the tomb, they did not find the body of the Lord Jesus.

In their bewilderment they were astonished to see a young man sitting on the right, and another standing by them, clothed in shining white robes. They were terrified, and bowed with faces to the ground.

But the angels said to the women: 'Don't be afraid, or astonished. We know you are looking for Jesus of Nazareth, the crucified one; why look for the living among the dead? He is not here because he has been raised, as he said; look, this is the place where they laid him.

'Remember what he said to you while you were still in Galilee: "The Son of Man must be delivered into the hands of sinful men, and be crucified, and on the third day rise again."'

They remembered those words.

'Now go quickly and tell Peter and the disciples that he has been raised from death, and that he is going ahead of you to Galilee. You will see him there, as he told you; and now I have told you too.'

(Matthew 28:1-7; Mark 16:1-7; Luke 24:1-8;
John 20:1-2)

The Women Tell the Apostles the Good News

The women came out of the tomb bewildered and trembling, and ran back with great fear and joy to report everything to the eleven and tell the news to the rest of his disciples. They said nothing to anyone on the way, because they were afraid.

Mary Magdalene ran to Simon Peter and the disciple Jesus loved, and said: 'They have taken the Lord out of the tomb, and we don't know where they have put him.' With her were Joanna, Mary the mother of James, and the others; they told the apostles everything.

To the apostles it seemed like nonsense; they didn't believe it. So Peter and the other disciple ran together to the tomb. The other ran faster and reached it first; bending down, he saw the linen sheets lying there, but did not go in.

Then Simon Peter came and went into the tomb. He saw the sheets, and also the cloth which had been around Jesus' head, not lying with the sheets but folded in another place. Then the disciple who had come first also went into the tomb, and he saw and believed. Until then, they had not understood the scripture that said he must rise again from death.

Then the disciples went back home.

(MATTHEW 28:8; MARK 16:8; LUKE 24:9–11; JOHN 20:2–10)

Jesus Shows Himself to Mary Magdalene and the Other Women

Rising from death early on Sunday, Jesus showed himself first to Mary Magdalene from whom he had expelled seven demons. She had been standing weeping outside the tomb and then stooped to look into it, still weeping, and saw two angels in white sitting where the body of Jesus had lain, one at the head and one at the feet.

They said: 'Woman, why are you crying?' She answered: 'They have taken my Lord away, and I don't know where they have put him.' As she said this, she turned and saw Jesus standing there, but did not know it was he.

He said: 'Woman, why are you crying? Who are you looking for?' Thinking he was the gardener, she said: 'Sir, if you have taken him away, tell me where you have put him, and I will fetch him.'

Jesus said to her: 'Mary.' Then she turned and said to him in Hebrew: *Rabbuni,* which means 'Teacher'.

He said: 'Do not cling to me, because I have not yet ascended to the Father; but go to my brothers and tell them I am ascending to my Father and your Father, to my God and your God.'

Mary Magdalene went to the disciples, who had been mourning and weeping, and told them he was alive and that he had said these things to her. She said: 'I have seen the Lord.' But they did not believe her.

Jesus also showed himself to the other women, and said to them: 'Rejoice!' They grasped his feet and worshipped him, and he said: 'Don't be afraid. Tell my brothers to go into Galilee; they will see me there.'

(MATTHEW 28:9–10; MARK 16:9–11; JOHN 20:11–18)

THE OFFICIAL EXPLANATION

While they were going, some of the guards came into the city and told the chief priests everything that had happened.

After meeting and discussing the problem with the elders, they gave a large bribe to the soldiers, instructing them: 'Say that his disciples came at night and stole him while you were sleeping. If the governor hears about it, we will use our influence; you will have nothing to worry about.'

They took the money and did as they were told, and this is the story the Jews have spread abroad to this day.

(MATTHEW 28:11–15)

TWO DISCIPLES MEET THE RISEN CHRIST

On the same day he showed himself in a different way to two disciples who were walking to a country village called Emmaus, about seven miles from Jerusalem. As they were discussing all that had happened, Jesus himself came up and walked with them; but they were prevented from recognizing him.

He asked: 'What were you talking about while you walked?' They looked sad, and one of them named Cleopas answered: 'Are you the only stranger in Jerusalem who hasn't heard about the things that happened there the last few days?'

Jesus asked: 'What things?' They said: 'About Jesus the Nazarene. In the eyes of God and all the people he was a prophet, powerful in word and deed; but our chief priests and rulers handed him over to be condemned to death and crucified. We were hoping that he was the one who would redeem Israel.

'Besides that, it is now the third day since this happened, and some women among us have astonished us. They went to his tomb early this morning, but did not find his body; then they came and told us they had seen a vision of angels who said he was alive. Some of us went to the tomb and found it empty, as the women said; but they did not see him.'

Jesus said to them: 'Foolish men, so slow in heart to believe in all that the prophets said! Surely the Messiah had to suffer these things before he could enter his glory?' Then, starting with Moses and all the prophets, he explained to them everything in scripture that referred to himself.

They came to the village to which they were going. He seemed to want to go further, but they urged him: 'Stay with us; the day is over, it's almost evening.' So he went in to stay with them.

As he reclined with them at table, he took bread, said the blessing, broke it and handed it to them. And their eyes were opened, and they recognized him; but then he vanished from their sight.

They said to each other: 'Didn't our hearts burn within us as he spoke to us on the road, and explained the scriptures to us?' That very hour they got up and went back to Jerusalem, where they found the eleven together with the disciples, who were saying: 'The Lord really has been raised, and has shown himself to Simon.'

So the two told them what had happened on the road, and how Jesus became known to them in the breaking of bread; but even they did not believe them.

(Mark 16:12–13; Luke 24:13–35)

JESUS SHOWS HIMSELF TO THE APOSTLES

Early in the evening that same Sunday, while the disciples were discussing these things behind closed doors for fear of the Jews, Jesus came and stood among them and said: 'Peace be with you.'

Alarmed and terrified, they thought they were seeing a ghost. But he said to them: 'Why are you afraid? Why do doubts arise in your hearts? Here are my hands and feet: look, it is I.' And he showed them his hands and his side. He said: 'Feel me; a ghost doesn't have flesh and bones, as you can see I have.'

The disciples rejoiced to see the Lord, but in their amazement could hardly believe it. So he said to them: 'Have you any food here?' They gave him a piece of broiled fish, and he took it and ate it in front of them.

(LUKE 24:36–43; JOHN 20:19)

HE EMPOWERS THEM TO FORGIVE SINS

Then Jesus said to them again: 'Peace be with you. As the Father sent me, I am sending you.' When he had said this, he breathed on them and said: 'Receive the Holy Spirit. If you forgive anyone's sins, they are forgiven them; if you do not forgive them, they are not forgiven.'

(JOHN 20:21–3)

JESUS CONVINCES THOMAS

But Thomas, one of the twelve called the Twin, was not with them when Jesus came. The other disciples told him: 'We have seen the Lord,' but he said: 'Unless I see the wounds of the nails in his hands and put my finger into them, and put my hand into his side, I will never believe it.'

Eight days later, the eleven disciples were indoors again, Thomas among them, and the doors were shut. As they reclined at table, Jesus came and stood among them and showed himself to them and said: 'Peace be with you.' He reproached them for obstinacy and scepticism, because they had not believed those who saw him first after he had risen.

Then he said to Thomas: 'See, here are my hands; put your finger here. Put your hand into my side; stop doubting, and believe.' Thomas said: 'My Lord and my God!'

Jesus replied: 'Now that you have seen me, do you believe? Blessed are those who have not seen, and yet believe.'

(MARK 16:14; JOHN 20:24–9)

THE RISEN LORD AT THE LAKESIDE

he next time Jesus showed himself to his disciples was by the sea of Tiberias; this is how it happened.

Simon Peter, Thomas called the Twin, Nathanael from Cana in Galilee, the sons of Zebedee and two other disciples were together. Simon said to them: 'I'm going fishing'; they said: 'We're coming with you.' They went out and got into the boat; but that night they caught nothing.

Soon after dawn Jesus stood on the shore, but the disciples did not know it was Jesus. He said to them: 'Children, have you caught nothing?' They answered 'No.' So he said: 'Drop the net to starboard and you'll find a catch.' They did, and could no longer haul it in because it was so full.

Then the disciple Jesus loved said to Peter: 'It is the Lord.' Peter, who was naked, hearing that it was the Lord, put on a tunic and jumped into the sea. The others came on in the boat dragging the net; they were only about a hundred yards from shore.

When they got out of the boat they saw a charcoal fire with a fish cooking, and bread. Jesus said: 'Bring some of the fish you've just caught.' Simon Peter went aboard and dragged the net to land, full of big fish, a hundred and fifty three of them; and though there were so many, the net was not torn.

Jesus said: 'Come and have breakfast.' Then he went to fetch the bread and gave it to them, and also the fish. Not one of the disciples dared to ask who he was; they knew it was the Lord.

This was the third time Jesus showed himself to the disciples after he was raised from death.

(JOHN 21:1–14)

JESUS PREPARES PETER FOR HIS MINISTRY

When they had eaten breakfast, Jesus said to Simon Peter: 'Simon son of John, do you love me more than these others?' He answered: 'Yes, Lord; you know I love you.' Jesus said to him: 'Feed my lambs.'

Then he asked him a second time: 'Simon son of John, do you love me?' Peter said: 'Yes, Lord, you know that I love you.' Jesus said: 'Shepherd my sheep.'

A third time he asked: 'Simon son of John, do you love me?' Peter was grieved that he asked him a third time, and said: 'Lord, you know everything; you know I love you.' Jesus said to him: 'Feed my sheep.

'Most truly I tell you, when you were young, you put on your own belt and walked where you liked; but when you grow old, you will stretch out your hands, and someone else will put a belt round you and take you where you do not wish to go.' He said this to signify the kind of death by which Peter would give glory to God. Then he told him: 'Follow me.'

Peter turned and saw, following them, the disciple Jesus loved, the one who had leaned on his breast at the supper and said: 'Lord, who is the one who will betray you?' So Peter asked Jesus: 'Lord, what about him?' Jesus answered: 'If I want him to stay till I come, what is that to you? You follow me.'

So a rumour went around the brothers that this disciple would not die; but Jesus did not say to him that he would not die. He said: 'If I want him to stay till I come, what is that to you?'

(JOHN 21:1–23)

JESUS SENDS HIS APOSTLES ON THEIR MISSION

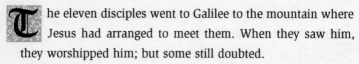 he eleven disciples went to Galilee to the mountain where Jesus had arranged to meet them. When they saw him, they worshipped him; but some still doubted.

Jesus came and spoke to them. He said: 'All authority in heaven and on earth has been given to me. Go therefore into all the world and proclaim the gospel to all creation. Make disciples of all the nations, baptizing them in the name of the Father and of the Son and of the Holy Spirit, teaching them to observe everything I have commanded you. Whoever believes and is baptized will be saved, but the one who will not believe will be condemned.

'These miracles will accompany those who believe. In my name they will expel demons, speak new languages and handle snakes; when they drink deadly poison, it will not harm them at all, and when they lay their hands on sick people they will recover; because I will always be with you, until the end of time.'

And he said: 'Remember what I told you while I was still with you: everything written about me in the law of Moses, the prophets and the psalms must be fulfilled.' He opened their minds to understand the scriptures, and said: 'So it was written that the Messiah would suffer, and rise again from death on the third day; and that in his name repentance for the forgiveness of sins would be proclaimed to all the nations, beginning from Jerusalem.

'You are witnesses of these things. I will send upon you the one my Father promised, so stay in the city until you are clothed with power from on high.'

(MATTHEW 28:16–20; MARK 16:15–18; LUKE 24:44–9)

OUR LORD'S ASCENSION INTO HEAVEN

After saying these things, the Lord Jesus led them out towards Bethany. Lifting up his hands, he blessed them and withdrew from them. As they watched, he was taken up into heaven to sit at God's right hand, and a cloud received him from their sight.

While they were gazing up to heaven, two men in white clothes came and stood beside them and said: 'Men of Galilee, why do you stand looking up to heaven? This Jesus who has been taken up from you to heaven will return in the same way you have seen him go.'

They returned to Jerusalem with great joy, and went about preaching everywhere, while the Lord worked with them, confirming their preaching by the miracles that accompanied it. And they were continually in the temple blessing God.

(MARK 16:19–20; LUKE 24:50–53; ACTS 1:9–11)

THIS IS NOT ALL THAT JESUS DID

This is the disciple who has written and testified about these things, and we know that his testimony is true. There were many other signs and wonders which Jesus did in the presence of the disciples, which are not written in this book; if every one were recorded, I think the world itself would not hold all the books that would have to be written.

But these have been written so that you may believe that Jesus is the Messiah, the Son of God, and believing this, have life in his name.

(JOHN 20:30–31; 21:24–5)

PRINCIPAL CHARACTERS
IN THE GOSPEL

JOHN THE BAPTIST

Dressed like Elijah and preaching in the desert, John announced the Messiah and the coming kingdom of God. He made crowds confess and repent of their sins and baptized them for forgiveness.

When Jesus came to him, John proclaimed him the Messiah who would baptize with the Holy Spirit and fire, and become the sacrificial lamb who atoned for the sins of the world.

John was no reed shaken by the wind, no slave to trends, and did not seek popularity. He was radical and anti-establishment, told people exactly what they had to stop doing, and warned of the wrath to come.

He told Herod the ruler of Galilee, who had divorced his wife and married his half-brother's, that he was living in sin. For this Herod imprisoned John, and Herodias had him killed.

Jesus said no greater man than John had ever been born.

MARY THE MOTHER OF JESUS

Mary exemplifies faith and humility. Committed to remaining a virgin, she nevertheless believed that by the power of the Holy Spirit she would become the mother of God's Son, the long-awaited Messiah.

She bore him among animals and laid him in their feeding-trough. She marvelled when mysterious magi did him homage and Simeon called him a light for the gentiles, warning that a sword would pierce her soul.

Their relationship was that of any mother and son, though he made it clear that faith in him outweighed blood relationship. She reacted like any mother when he slipped away at the age of twelve to do his Father's business, but normally he obeyed his parents, and a hint from Mary moved him to perform his first miracle.

Separated from Jesus during his public life, she saw him suffer and die, after he had entrusted her to the disciple he loved.

JOSEPH THE HUSBAND OF MARY

Joseph respected Mary's commitment to virginity and agreed to a marriage of companionship and protection, until he learned of her pregnancy. But he came to believe it was miraculous, and so became the foster-father of Jesus.

As descendants of David they travelled to Bethlehem, where Jesus was born, for a census. An angel warned Joseph to save him from Herod's massacre. In Nazareth he taught his son his carpenter's trade.

Each Passover he took his family to Jerusalem; when Jesus was twelve, he stayed there after his parents left for home. Missing him in their group, they went back and found him among the teachers in the temple; he said he had work to do for his Father in heaven. Then he returned to Nazareth and was obedient to them.

Joseph seems to have died before Jesus began to preach.

SIMON PETER

Impetuous but warm-hearted, Simon became the apostles' leader and spokesman. Jesus named him Rock (Greek *Petros,* Peter), and said he would build his church on this rock; he promised Peter the keys of God's kingdom and guidance in declaring his decrees.

When Jesus foretold his crucifixion and Peter protested, Jesus answered: 'Get behind me, Satan [tempter]. You are an obstacle to me because you think about human things, not the things of God.'

Having boasted he would die with Jesus, Peter was so frightened by his arrest that he denied knowing him. After he repented, Jesus again gave him the task of shepherding his flock and strengthening his brothers in faith.

His ministry, death and burial at Rome are attested by tradition. He was executed during Nero's reign on the Vatican, the site of his tomb.

ANDREW

Compared with his impetuous brother Simon, Andrew seems calm and controlled. Born in Bethsaida near Capernaum, both were fishermen on the sea of Galilee and friends of James and John.

Andrew had been a follower of John the Baptist, through whom he met Jesus. He brought Simon to Jesus, and they gave up fishing to be with him constantly. Andrew is always listed among the four disciples closest to Jesus.

Tradition says he later preached in Bithynia, Scythia, Macedonia and Achaia and that he was crucified in Patras about AD 70. He is often shown with an X-shaped cross, though this may be a misunderstanding of a legend.

Devotion to St Andrew spread from Greece to Rome in the fifth century and from there to France and England. He is the patron saint of Russia and Scotland, and has a feast day in his honour on 30 November.

JAMES THE ELDER

Two apostles were called James. The older James and his brother John were fishermen, friends of Simon Peter and his brother Andrew.

Jesus called them 'sons of thunder' for their youthful ardour and zeal; they once wanted to call down fire from heaven on some inhospitable Samaritans. When their mother asked

Jesus to give them positions of honour in his kingdom, he promised instead that they would share his suffering.

James is listed among the four apostles closest to Jesus; he was with him when he healed Peter's mother-in-law and brought Jairus's daughter back to life, saw him in glory at his transfiguration, and in agony as he prayed before his arrest.

James was put to the sword by order of Herod Agrippa about AD 44, before any of the gospels were written.

JOHN

The other impetuous 'son of thunder' was rebuked with his brother when their mother asked Jesus to give them special positions in his kingdom. But he too accompanied Jesus when other disciples were left behind, and in his gospel calls himself only 'the disciple Jesus loved'.

He was at the foot of the cross when the dying Jesus said to Mary his mother: 'Woman, this is your son,' and to John, 'this is your mother'. From that day he took her into his home.

Though a fisherman, John had some formal education, and with Peter and James became a pillar of the church in Jerusalem until he left for Ephesus. Exiled to Patmos during Domitian's persecution, he wrote his apocalypse. After Domitian's death he returned to Ephesus and wrote a gospel consisting largely of material not contained in the other three.

He died a natural death at a great age, perhaps in AD 104.

JUDAS ISCARIOT

For the price of a slave and because Jesus would not lead a revolution, Judas led his captors to him at night, since they would not arrest him publicly.

He understood that the kingdom Jesus proclaimed would bring neither political liberation nor wealth to his apostles. Judas also showed greed and lack of conscience; he stole from the common purse Jesus shared with his disciples.

But when Jesus was condemned, Judas repented, threw away the thirty pieces of silver and hanged himself – not the behaviour of an ordinary mercenary. Though he loved money he loved Jesus too, and betrayed him with a kiss as if he couldn't bear to point and say: 'That's the one.'

Perhaps St John's explanation is best: Satan entered him. His final tragedy was that when he remembered his master's last warning, 'better for him if he had never been born', he believed he could never be forgiven.

PONTIUS PILATE

As governor of Judaea Pilate showed contempt for his subjects. He used temple funds to build an aqueduct and crushed the ensuing riots; he brought standards bearing the emperor's image into Jerusalem, only removing them after six days of protests.

But he had a sense of justice and law, and tried to save Jesus from death, though not to the point of risking his career.

He saw that the charges against Jesus – that he claimed to be a king, refused taxes to Caesar and was stirring up rebellion – were not the real reason the chief priests wanted him dead.

Illogically he ruled that though he found Jesus guilty of no crime, he would have him scourged before releasing him. But the mob shouted for his crucifixion, so Pilate washed his hands of him. He took a small revenge with a title on the cross: 'Jesus of Nazareth, King of the Jews.'

MARY MAGDALENE

ome imagine that Jesus and Mary of Magdala were lovers; others confuse her with the penitent who washed his feet with tears and dried them with her hair.

In fact Mary was one of several women who provided Jesus and his closest disciples with food, domestic help and other necessities at their own expense.

Having witnessed his crucifixion and burial, Mary was the first to see him alive again and mistook him for a gardener. 'Sir,' she said, 'if you have taken him away, tell me where you have put him, and I will fetch him' – but she recognized him when he spoke her name. 'Don't cling to me,' he said; 'I have still to ascend to the Father.'

Mary Magdalene ran to tell the disciples that Jesus had risen, but they didn't believe her. Only after Jesus had showed himself to the other women did his disciples see him.

ISRAEL IN THE TIME OF JESUS

I srael has seldom been politically unified and independent. In the time of Jesus, it was part of the Roman empire. Soon after he was born, its vassal king Herod the Great died, willing his kingdom to his three sons.

Archelaus took over Judaea, Samaria and Idumaea – half the kingdom. He ruled autocratically until the Jews sent leading men to Rome to protest. He was banished in AD 6, and from then on his territory was administered by Roman procurators, among them Pontius Pilate who ruled from 26 to 36.

Herod's second son, Antipas, ruled Galilee and Peraea as a tetrarch – someone who rules a fourth part of a kingdom. He was vain and lazy, and cunning: Jesus called him 'that fox'. His downfall began when he divorced his wife, the daughter of King Aretas of Nabataea, in favour of Herodias the wife of his half-brother; John the Baptist was put to death for denouncing the affair, but Aretas avenged the insult by defeating Antipas in a border dispute. The emperor Caligula exiled him two years later.

The third son, Philip, originally married to Herodias, became tetrarch of Trachonitis, Ituraea and adjacent regions from AD 4 to 34, and proved a just and benevolent ruler.

THE HIGH PRIEST AND THE GREAT SANHEDRIN

In theory the high priest was the nation's head, and in certain periods he wielded much of the power of a king. The sanhedrin or council over which he presided played a leading role in Israel's religious and national life.

Though tradition attributed it to Moses, the sanhedrin arose as a limited form of self-government granted by foreign rulers. Herod the Great stripped it of real power, but the procurators restored it in Judaea at least; Rome believed in allowing conquered peoples a measure of self-government.

Among its seventy-one members one group was made up of former high priests and senior members of their families; another represented the lay aristocracy of wealthy or influential citizens, and a third the scribes or doctors of the law.

The sanhedrin could judge any religious or civil case according to Jewish law, and under the procurators its decisions could be enforced by its own police or that of the Romans. It could pass the death sentence, but not execute it without confirmation by the Roman magistrate. It had rules of procedure which determined when it could meet, how evidence was heard, and how it voted and passed sentence; but the trial of Jesus, for which it first met at night in the high priest's house, showed that exceptions could be made.

THE TEMPLE AND ITS PRIESTS

The temple in Jerusalem was where God lived among his people in a unique way, and by the time of Jesus it had become the only place where Jews offered sacrifice. Solomon built the first temple, destroyed by Nebuchadnezzar of Babylon in 586 BC; a second was built after the Babylonian exile and dedicated in 515, and Herod the Great demolished that one to build the temple in which Jesus taught. He began in 19 BC, but decoration was not finished till AD 64, six years before the Romans destroyed it.

Sacrifices or gifts to God are an act of worship found in most religions. Jewish sacrifices acknowledged that all creation belongs to God, or represented the punishment men deserve for disobeying his laws; they could be a prayer for God's forgiveness, or a way of thanking him for favours.

One who offered a sacrificial animal laid his hand on its head; then its throat was cut and the priest gave its lifeblood back to God by pouring it around the altar or sprinkling or smearing it on the altar. In the most solemn kind of sacrifice, a holocaust, the victim was then burned to ashes in the fire on the altar.

Another kind, the communion sacrifice, was sometimes called a thanksgiving – eucharist in the Greek old testament. Parts of a lamb were burned on the altar, but the rest was boiled and eaten by the priest, the one who offered it and his family and guests. Since it was now the lamb of God, God fed them as a father feeds his children around his table, nourishing their intimacy with him and one another.

Only a priest (*kohen*) could offer the blood of sacrificed animals or burn them on the altar. Priests were members of a special clan within the tribe of Levi, set apart from ordinary activities for the service of God. A priest was a mediator between God and man; in early times he was also a teacher of the law and an oracle who discerned the will of God, but these functions had been taken over by scribes and prophets.

Other members of the tribe of Levi, called simply Levites, held administrative posts in the temple or were singers or instrumentalists or looked after the sacred vessels. The nearest they came to acting as priests was when they slaughtered sacrificial victims.

SADDUCEES AND PHARISEES

Both Sadducees and Pharisees believed that true religion rested on the Torah or law God had given through Moses, but they disagreed about its extent.

The Sadducees, mostly the priestly aristocracy and its supporters, rejected the Pharisees' belief in angels, spirits and the resurrection of the dead as innovations, and claimed that they alone preserved Israel's ancient heritage.

The Pharisees arose out of popular opposition to Greek culture when it began to influence Israel in the second century BC. Many Jews, hating anything foreign and calling themselves *hasidim* (pious), rebelled against the policy of their kings who favoured accommodations to Hellenism.

But when their own representatives came to the throne they could not avoid political relations with the Hellenic world or stop the infiltration of Greek culture. They began to oppose the *hasidim* and drew their support from the priestly and aristocratic classes. Hassidic Jews regarded them as traitors, and some began keeping apart from everything they considered irreligious or impure, calling themselves 'separated' – in Aramaic *perishayya*, Pharisees.

Then their conflict with the Sadducees became a doctrinal one. Sadducees would accept only the written law as authoritative, while the Pharisees appealed to complementary traditions. They held that God had given Moses not only the written Torah but an oral law, expressed in traditional precepts that governed every aspect of life. Their commentaries developed into a vast legal system that gained more practical importance than the written law; and as Jesus pointed out, what they regarded as a protective fence around the law could even contradict it.

The Sadducees regarded the doctrines Pharisees drew from the oral law as distortions of the ancient Hebrew spirit of which they considered themselves the guardians; but the people admired the Pharisees.

THE SCRIBES

The gospel often pairs scribes and Pharisees together, though not every Pharisee was a scribe; a scribe was a teacher of the law, a scholar and intellectual. He could be priest or layman, Sadducee or Pharisee, but by the time of Jesus most scribes were Pharisees.

For a Jew, knowledge of the law was the highest learning. As early as the Babylonian exile some devoted their lives to its study, earning the title Rab or Rabbi ('master', 'my master'). By taking over the work of teaching that had once belonged to the priests, the scribes became the spiritual fathers of the people, their catechists and moral guides and the preachers in their synagogues.

ZEALOTS

The Zealots, mostly Pharisees, were nationalists ready to fight for the principle that no one but God could rule his chosen people. They opposed paying taxes to Caesar, and saw the census of Judaea in AD 6–7 as a sacrilegious gentile imposition. It provoked Judas the Galilean to lead a revolt which was put down by the Romans, but Zealots kept alive the opposition that erupted in the final Jewish rebellion of 66–70.

Meanwhile they sometimes assassinated foreigners and Jews they judged guilty of collaboration, using a short dagger the Romans called *sica*, which gave them the name *sicarii*. Most Jews disapproved of them, but among Jesus' disciples Simon was called a Zealot.

ESSENES

The gospel does not mention Essenes, but from the second century BC they formed religious communities in several places, notably at Qumran on the western shore of the Dead Sea where the remains of an Essene centre and part of its library – the Dead Sea scrolls – have been found.

The Essenes expected the end of this world and the coming of the new Jerusalem. Their communities included priests, and their way of life resembled later Christian monasticism. Those who lived in community seem to have practised celibacy. Days were divided between prayer and work under strict obedience to a written rule, new members gave their property to the community and all earnings went into a common treasury.

The Essenes had little influence on mainstream Judaism, but some adopted Essene ideas and imitated their way of life.

NOTES

1 Matthew selects names so that there are, as he says, fourteen generations each between Abraham, David, the deportation to Babylon and the birth of Christ. Luke starts with Adam and adds a parallel line through Nathan, Solomon's brother.

2 Descent could be legal rather than natural. The law of Moses ruled that when a man died childless, his brother should marry his widow, and their first child would take the dead man's name (Deuteronomy 25:5-10). Julius Africanus, writing in Israel in the third century, records the tradition that Joseph had two fathers, as shown here, because Heli died childless and his half brother Jacob married his widow.

3 The Bible is the word of God in the words of men. Jesus would have made his meaning clear, but Matthew's and Luke's versions of this saying are not clear to modern commentators; this free translation represents what some of them think Jesus said.

4 Luke emphasizes that the gentile centurion appealed to Jesus through others, almost as though he were correcting Matthew

who did not know this. Matthew does not contradict Luke, but records what happened as though the centurion himself spoke to Jesus.

5 Matthew and Luke say Jesus told them not to take a staff, while Mark makes him say they should; Matthew says he told them not to take sandals, but Mark makes him say they should wear them. It seems clear that our Lord forbade only a *second* staff or pair of sandals, just as he told them not to take two tunics. All three versions mean the same: they were to have only what they needed at the moment.

6 Other versions of St John's gospel add: 'Because an angel of the Lord came down into the pool at certain times and stirred up the water; and the first person to go into the water after this disturbance was cured of whatever disease he was suffering from.'

7 Whatever Matthew and Luke may have thought, Jesus cannot have meant he would come in glory in the lifetime of his hearers, but that he would come in the church which is his body and a partial manifestation of God's kingdom. They would see its powerful growth even under persecution; they would also not taste death as the end of life, but as a share in his passion and resurrection.

8 God's name for himself. We have existence, but he is existence, infinite and eternal. We are to call him Yahweh, WHO IS.

9 Luke's word is 'hate', but our Lord does not allow us to wish evil to anyone. He means we must rise above every tie of blood, love or affection when the gospel demands it.

10 Jesus teaches that divorce is not merely wrong but ineffective; divorced people are still married in God's eyes, or their second marriages would not be adultery.

11 Matthew and Mark say they were leaving Jericho, and Luke that they were coming near Jericho; but there were two Jerichos. People still lived near the ruins of the ancient city whose walls were flattened in Joshua's day; Jesus would have been leaving there and coming near the modern city, partly built by Herod the Great and his son Archelaus, when he came upon Bartimaeus. Only Matthew tells us that Bartimaeus was accompanied by another blind man, who seems to have been less vocal.

12 St Matthew's word is 'comes', but this is not the coming of the Son of Man to judge us at the end of the world; rather, it was his coming as the judge of those who had rejected him when Jerusalem and the temple were destroyed in AD 70. 'These things' at the end of this section refer to the same destruction.

13 As God he knows everything, but as far as we are concerned even he does not know this, since it is no part of his mission to reveal it.

14 This is like the parable on page 164; it seems that our Lord adapted it to a different audience or different circumstances.

15 The Father is greater in the sense that he sent his Son to do his will by becoming one of us and suffering for us. But the divine greatness of the Father and the Son is one and the same, infinite and incomparable.

16 That is, Annas

17 Our codices of St John's gospel say 'about the sixth hour', or noon, but Mark says Jesus was nailed to the cross at the third hour, nine o'clock. A copying mistake is not impossible; but John may have been counting the hours from midnight as was done in the west, or Mark may have meant between nine and noon.

18 Not Jesus' own despairing question, but the first line of Psalm
   22 which describes how he suffered on the cross and was
   taunted, and foretells his future glory.

19 Matthew and Mark say a reed; John has hyssop, which may be
   a mistake for *hysso*, a soldier's pike.